# CLOSE CALLS

## CLIMBING MISHAPS & NEAR-DEATH EXPERIENCES

## John Long

FALCON®

HELENA, MONTANA

You can order extra copies of this book and get information and prices for other Falcon® books by writing Falcon, P.O. Box 1718, Helena, MT 59624 or calling toll free 1-800-582-2665. Also, please ask for a free copy of our current catalog. Visit our website at www.FalconOutdoors.com or contact us via e-mail at falcon@falcon.com.

Library of Congress Cataloging-in-Publication Data

Long, John.
    Close calls: climbing mishaps and near-death experiences
    / by John Long; illustrations by Tami Knight
    p. cm.
    Includes bibliographical references.
    ISBN 1-56044-762-1 (pbk.)
    1. Rock climbing accidents. 2. Near-death experiences.
    I. Title. II. Series.
    GV200.2.L64 1999
    796.52'23'0289--dc21                                 99-25925
                                                CIP

**CAUTION**

Outdoor recreational activities are by their very nature potentially hazardous. All participants in such activities must assume responsibility for their own actions and safety. The information contained in this book cannot replace sound judgment and good decision-making skills, which help reduce risk exposure, nor does the scope of this book allow for disclosure of all the potential hazards and risks involved in such activities.

Learn as much as possible about the outdoor recreational activities in which you participate, prepare for the unexpected, and be cautious. The reward will be a safer and more enjoyable experience.

 Text pages printed on recycled paper.

# TABLE OF CONTENTS

1. SOFT AS CHURCH MUSIC .................................. 5
*Touched by an angel on a Valley classic*

2. A MAUDLIN MOMENT ON HALF DOME ........................... 7
*"Even if it kills us both!"*

3. THE RUNNING (AWAY) BELAY ............................. 10
*"No-Pro Bill" bolts from the bugs*

4. THE DEVIL VISITS ANGEL FALLS ........................ 12
*Californians nearly washed into Next World*

5. RABBI GUNTHER SAYS "ENOUGH!" ........................ 16
*He surely fudged on his Kosher diet*

6. MADNESS ON THE SPIRE ............................. 20
*Under the knife on Lost Arrow*

7. LOVE ON THE CLIFFSIDE ........................ 23
*Love strikes twice on infamous Yosemite outing*

8. WILLIAM W'S WONDROUS WRENCHER ................... 25
*Willoughby wheezed, whimpered, and whistled off*

9. MEXICAN INDULGENCE ......................... 27
*Why do you think they call it dope?*

10. MAD WAVES AND ENGLISHMEN ................... 30
*Taking the royal bath*

11. AFFAIR OF THE MALEVOLENT "CHAMBERPOT" ............ 32
*Tallywhacker sliced to the quick in the High Cascades*

12. RESCUE TEAM TACKLES THE FALLS .................. 34
*Just who sold that man a knife?!*

13. LIGHTS ALMOST OUT ON INSOMNIA .................... 36
*"Acapulco Dave" dives again*

14. ASS-DRAGGED IN WISCONSIN ....................... 39
*The Devil (in the lake) made him do it*

15. TOOTH AND NAIL IN ARCO ...................... 42
*Hal chews the cord*

16. "FORE!" .............................. 44
*Teeing off on El Capitan*

17. KUNG FU ON WASHINGTON COLUMN ................................ 46
*Ugly American gets his clock cleaned*

18. NELLIE'S NIGHT OUT .............................................. 48
*Yosemite hardman learns the meaning of being "cut off"*

19. PRUSIK GRABS LIKE GRIM DEATH .............................. 50
*Bess left dangling in thin air*

20. FOR NUTS ONLY ..................................................... 52
*"Raked with a bastard file"*

21. INSUFFICIENTLY HUSKY .......................................... 55
*Jammed line on the Whiteout*

22. SWISS GRIPPED ON THE DOME ................................. 57
*"Sheest! Dees line is bullsheet!"*

23. DIVING OFF THE CAPTAIN ........................................ 59
*Saved by the hand of God*

24. HIKERS FILCH THORNTON'S LINE ............................. 61
*Sun nearly sets on Sunshine Wall*

25. RODENTS RIP RUBY'S ROPE ...................................... 64
*Gnawed to the quick on the Big Stone*

26. DOG DAYS AT SMITH ROCKS .................................... 67
*"Horny" had a hunger*

27. GRANITE PINBALL .................................................. 68
*Bombs away on the East Buttress*

28. NO KNOT ON THE NOSE .......................................... 71
*Rock stars make do with nothing*

29. GERTY SKIDS THE PLANK ........................................ 74
*Blazing buns on Captain Hook*

30. FERDY'S FINGERS BUTTER OFF ................................. 76
*Tarred and feathered but still kicking*

31. NABISCO FLYER ..................................................... 78
*Ozzie takes the swing*

32. HELLUVA TIME ON MT. DUTZI ................................. 79
*"Blockhead" Lucifer and the desert serpent*

33. LUCKY SKIPS THE CLIP .......................................... 82
*Lucky logs a fall*

34. DOPE ON THE TOPROPE ........................................... 84
*"He carved through space like a trapeze geek"*

35. WINCHED OFF THE DECK.................................... 86
*They smacked like clackers*

36. HANK FELT "STRONG LIKE BULL" ........................ 88
*. . . Then the hold spun*

37. WHEN LANGSTON LOST IT ................................. 90
*Ankles away on the Gunnite Roof*

38. THROBBING PATE ............................................ 92
*Dead head from the deadpoint*

39. FRANK'S FACE FRACTURED IN FLYING FIASCO................ 94
*They met by chance in midair*

40. RUNNING THE ROPE IN TUOLOMNE MEADOWS.................. 97
*Ginny's gain is Vinny's pain*

41. LIGHTNING STRIKES THE ARROWHEAD ..................... 99
*Haste wastes Nate's hands*

42. BULLY'S COMEUPPANCE ..................................... 102
*Rediscovering the karma connection*

43. LOST LINE................................................... 105
*What we've got here is a failure to communicate*

44. MISHAP AT MATTRESS QUARRY ........................... 107
*Skydiving into the slag heap*

45. SEAMUS YANKS TOO HARD ................................. 108
*Jules "barked like a dog"*

46. RALPH'S RUGGED RAP ..................................... 110
*He slid down the line like a bead on a string*

47. "SUGAR" LOST HER LOAD ................................. 112
*Roland should have known*

48. NIGHTMARE ON SEA OF DREAMS ......................... 114
*Their teeth chattered like those wind-up dentures*

49. DOWNWARD BOUND ........................................ 118
*The day the slings gave way*

50. RED ALERT! ................................................ 120
*Natasha crashes like Sputnik*

51. SHIVERING ON THE SPIRE ................................ 122
*"The rope slid through the anchors!"*

52. ASTEROIDS FLY ON ASTROMAN ........................... 124
*Ned gets nailed upside the head*

53. HELL IN ELDORADO .................................................. 127
*Violet needed elbow room*

54. CURLY JOE TAKES A SHORTCUT ........................ 129
*Moe cracks his melon*

55. INADEQUATE CORDAGE ..................................... 133
*Monty's left marooned in high mountain mess*

56. HERBERT CALLS THE SHOT .............................. 135
*Herbie comes up short*

57. "HOLY S#%T!" ...................................................... 137
*Upton goes upside down*

58. FROZEN IN THE BOMBAY DOOR ..................... 140
*"If he popped, they both were goners . . ."*

59. THE SKIES PART ON ORKNEY .......................... 143
*Save a penny, spend a shilling*

60. JOE SPILLS THE JO ............................................. 146
*Nasty burn on Jasper's ass*

61. "COURAGE IN A CAN" ........................................ 148
*The ground wins . . . again*

62. FROZEN STIFF ON WHITNEY ............................ 150
*Gus flashes back to Hades*

63. HARD TIMES AT THE HAGGERMEISTERS ........ 152
*The hatefully hopeless toprope*

64. NOT THE KNOT TED NEEDED ........................... 155
*Ted and Alice left high and dry*

65. ROY SEES SIGFRIED FLY ................................... 158
*The jugs flew off the rope*

66. LARRY LEAP-FROGS ALOT ................................ 161
*The rusty, manky, mauled, and entirely shabby fixed 1" angle came out!*

67. "DUSTED" ON DESPAIR ..................................... 163
*Freddy flails, flops from classic flare*

68. MIRACLE ON FRUSTRATION ............................. 166
*Yabbo dives for deliverance*

# PREFACE

I received much of this material—especially the hilarious entries—in freeze-dried form. I've mixed it with a little water here and there to add some body. In other words, I haven't hesitated to have fun with the text whenever the chance presented itself—and sometimes when it didn't. I hope readers have as much fun reading these accounts as I often had writing them.

Future volumes of this work may be produced, and readers are invited to submit their own close calls to: Close Calls, c/o Falcon Publishing, P.O. Box 1718, Helena, MT 59624; or e-mail them to: closecalls@falcon.com.

Safe & Happy Climbing!

John Long

# INTRODUCTION

I've always been of two minds concerning close calls and climbing mishaps: one mind says that, since climbing could kill me every time out, eventually the odds will catch up with me. A hanging-belay anchor will blow out, or a giant block will dislodge above and come crashing down on me and . . . dust to dust. The other mind insists that the greater my experience, the sooner I'll recognize potential trouble and be able to steer clear.

The unsettling part is that neither mind is absolutely true or false.

Naturally, we all want to know what the score is, but the score is never certain until each climb is behind us. And the score from yesterday never carries over to today. Luck is a factor. So is alertness, fatigue, and—as several of the following cases illustrate—fluke. But arguably the most important thing to understand is that a climber's fate rests largely in his or her own hands. And even the most experienced climbers occasionally make fundamental errors in judgment and technique.

Consider the hundreds of people I've known who have climbed for ten or more years. Nearly all can relate incidents that could have killed them but did not. Never mind zippering a string of A4 pins, or pinging off an unprotected lieback—I'm talking about El Cap veterans rappelling off the end of their ropes, having their harnesses come untied, and a score of other novice blunders. Every year "acts of God" (lightning, rockfall, etc.) retire a handful of climbers. But such events are surprisingly rare. Statistics say that most climbing injuries are avoidable. Gravity is unforgiving and does not discriminate between the hacker and the world-class ace. At the bottom of the crag, we all start up as equals.

Reading about climbing accidents and close calls will always rivet us, for the sweat is cold and the horrors are real. But for practicing climbers, the instructional value often outweighs the human-interest factor. It's important to remember that even the most mundane mishaps—slip-ups we cringe at momentarily but then quickly forget—could just as easily have been fatal, had luck not been on our side. The stories that follow are reminders of what can go wrong in the vertical world, and there's nothing that drives the point home better than short anecdotes about real-life climbers on actual climbs. That is the focus of this book.

The format is simple: I've collected accounts of close calls and a few genuine accidents, related the stories in bullet form, then reviewed the scenarios to determine what went wrong and how climbers might avoid repeating the mishaps. In many cases the business is cut and dry. In others we find ourselves on slippery ground, especially when judgment is required, as it normally is. The variations in the climbing experience are too diverse for pat solutions to apply across the slab. In the gray areas, the most we can hope for is awareness of those circumstances that require our extreme vigilance; this in itself is our best defense against accidents.

The source for these accounts came from personal experiences and those told to me by friends and acquaintances; others were solicited over the internet; still others were culled from national park records. Because some contributors requested anonymity, I've gone with pseudonyms rather than actual names. Oftentimes I've foregone (or changed) specific times, dates, route names and so forth. This is not a history book or a source of official statistics, and I didn't want to swindle readers into believing vital lessons could be found in trivia germane to a police report.

The importance, I believe, is in learning why an accident occurred and how we might avoid repeating it—not on the same route, of course, but when we encounter similar conditions. The key here is, "similar conditions." Experts disagree on this point. Some insist that exhaustive examination of specific incidents best illustrates the tangible stuff with which people can really learn about safety. I agree—so long as we are talking about THAT particular incident. But too much focus on the specifics of, say, how the rope got hung up on the fifteenth pitch of *Tis-sa-ack* is of less overall value than looking at a specific incident to learn how ropes generally get hung up and searching for the common denominators that the specifics suggest. So I've used the specific to go to the general, believing the real issue is how to avoid getting our ropes hung up, not how to avoid getting our rope hung up on the fifteenth pitch of *Tis-sa-ack*.

On the long road to mastery, we all make mistakes. Some of us pay dearly for a minor oversight; others seem destined to live through anything. Yet it is said that Luck tires from carrying anyone too long on her shoulders. We can't change our own fortune, but we can increase our awareness of situations in which accidents are likely to occur, or bad luck is likely to strike. And we can familiarize ourselves with the mistakes that, once made, cannot be reversed by all the luck in the world. Ultimately, the majority of close calls involve luck in one way alone: a climber made an avoidable error and lived to talk about it. The purpose of this manual is to raise our understanding to that place where knowledge, not luck, will save our day.

# 1

# SOFT AS CHURCH MUSIC

*Touched by an angel on a Valley classic*

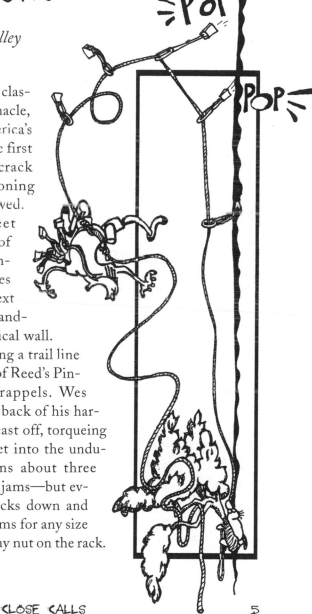

Les and Wes set out to bag the classic *Center Route* on Reed's Pinnacle, Yosemite, one of North America's most storied 5.10s. Les led the first pitch, a sixty-foot curving crack (5.9) ending at a tree festooning from the precipice. Wes followed. At the belay, with his feet stretched out on the branches of the tree—and piss ants swarming all over his bare legs—Wes quickly racked up for the next lead, a wavy, 120-foot 5.10 handcrack splitting a flawless, vertical wall.

The team had brought along a trail line to facilitate retreat off the top of Reed's Pinnacle, which requires two rappels. Wes clipped the trail line onto the back of his harness, drew a deep breath and cast off, torqueing his hands and twisting his feet into the undulating fissure. The crack runs about three inches wide—too fat for hand jams—but every two feet or so it bottlenecks down and affords perfect, form-fitting jams for any size hand and ideal slots for most any nut on the rack.

But the climbing is unrelenting, and the fatigue factor tends to exert itself suddenly.

About fifty feet up the pitch, Wes's arms filled with lead. He huffed; he screamed; he whistled off. Pitching down the sheer wall, his string of seemingly bombproof nuts shot from the crack. His body hurtled past Les, who was cringing in the tree—and then came a sharp report, like a bullwhip. The tree crackled and popped; gaping down, Les saw his partner flip upside down and decelerate as if on the end of a bungee cord, then watched as Wes's head gently kissed the rocky ground and he eased to a stop, soft as church music. Wes righted himself and stood up, his feet just barely touching the deck, his body still suspended by the trail line that had wrapped itself miraculously around the branches of the tree, arresting his certain death-fall.

COMMENTARY: This episode, one of the most famous to ever come out of Yosemite, is not only an example of transcendental luck, but living proof that a crack branded "idiot proof" (so far as accepting bombproof nuts) ain't necessarily so.

PREVENTION: The mystery here is—how did the nuts possibly fail when every placement was in a virtual bottleneck? I've climbed this pitch many times and know that anything from a medium Stopper to a #10 hex can seat tightly almost anywhere in the crack. But one thing demands attention: the sling on the nut must never be thicker than the crack immediately below the placement. Neglect this crucial point and the sling does not pass through the bottleneck, but lies over it. When shock-loaded, the pull on the otherwise bomber nut is not down—in the direction of loading—but rather out. This is the only conceivable explanation as to how all the nuts pulled from a crack famous for immediate and bomber placements.

# 2.

# A MAUDLIN MOMENT ON HALF DOME

*"Even if it kills us both!"*

For well nigh ten years, Danny had dreamed about climbing Half Dome. However, owing to a cranky, demanding nature, partners were hard for Danny to come by. Twice Danny schlepped up to the great gray face, and twice Danny never got off the deck. (The first sortie ended in a fistfight when Danny insisted his partner fetch water and firewood, then organize the gear as Danny eyeballed the route.) Finally Danny drafted his cousin, Mac, a convicted felon fresh out of Sing Sing.

Only twenty-two, Mac had been an excellent high school athlete and presently resembled Mr. Olympia by virtue of a rigorous weight-training program he'd adopted in the Big House. Mac's formal climbing instruction included five expeditions to the Rockreation climbing gym in Costa Mesa, California, and a one-day crack-climbing seminar

at Tahquitz Rock followed by an afternoon jumaring a rope strung from a gigantic oak in Danny's front yard. Said training was accomplished in a ten-day stretch, after which Mac declared himself ready for "any goddam rock."

Danny and Mac were at the base of Half Dome the following weekend. A swift and efficient leader, Danny blazed up the initial, moderate pitches of the distinguished northwest face. Mac had learned his lessons well and followed like an old hand, not cowing, but rather marveling at the spectacle of dangling on the sheer palisades of the cloud-gathering dome. By late afternoon, the duo had dusted off seventeen pitches and were standing on Big Sandy Ledge, the standard bivouac site for fleet teams.

As Danny slowly settled in, he occasionally peered over the edge at the yawing void below, then gaped up at the terrible, jutting Visor, cantilevered off the lip of the summit so very far overhead. Soon he was overcome by a blue funk that quickly turned to terror. Mac, meanwhile, was milling about Big Sandy, huffing Camel straights, cranking the odd boulder problem on the wall behind them and wondering why they had "up and quit" with so much daylight left.

Later that night, Danny informed Mac that they would have to bail the next morning because he wasn't feeling so good. Mac wrote it off to nerves—he'd felt the same way before holding up his first 7-Eleven. He promised Danny the condition would pass. Danny assured Mac that they were going down, that he was done. Mac cracked his knuckles and assured Danny he would indeed be "done in" if he mentioned the going-down idea again—he, Mac, was climbing this rock come hell or high water and wasn't bailing simply because his cousin had "gone yellow." Danny could not argue with a confirmed bonecrusher like Mac, nor could he muster the mettle to lead another inch up the harrowing dome.

This proved not to be a problem, however, because the next morning Mac agreed to lead the team to glory. His training at Rockreation notwithstanding, Mac's only leading experience was the second pitch of the *Trough* (5.1) at Tahquitz, which he'd led during his crack-climbing class. Mac spent half the day cursing, trembling, hammering, and frigging his way up the two Zig-Zag pitches directly off Big Sandy Ledge. At this pace, they wouldn't top out till the following spring.

At the hanging belay atop the second Zig-Zag pitch, as Danny watched his cousin racking the gear in bleeding hands, something shifted in Danny's head when Mac, his hands quivering with fear and his voice cracking with emotion, confessed that he had botched everything in his life and that—goddamit!—he wasn't going to botch this climb, "even if it kills us both." As Danny describes it, he knew once and for all that they both needed this victory or they'd spend the rest of their sorry lives drinking rude liquors, spatting with women and kicking stray dogs. Danny drew a deep breath, spit for effect, grabbed the rack and cast off on the next lead—and kept leading all the way to the last pitch, which they gained at twilight. He offered Mac the courtesy of leading the team to the summit. After fumbling through a few A1 placements, Mac found the easy friction that led to the top of the dome and the deed was done.

COMMENTARY: Over the following ten years, Danny and Mac became inseparable partners and climbed over thirty-five grade VIs together, including trips up the most fearsome walls in the land. Presently the pair are painting contractors in Santa Monica, California.

PREVENTION: Such a trial by fire is not recommended. A big wall is not the place to learn the ropes. Not often do two Phoenixes rise from the ashes of a big wall meltdown and hammer their way to glory.

# 3

# THE RUNNING (AWAY) BELAY

*"No-Pro Bill" bolts from the bugs*

Toproping is a main game in the Midwest climbing scene, and folks quickly acquire a penchant for unanchored belays much as a young farm hand learns to tether unbroken steeds. The hike to the crag is usually trivial—often paved. On a given weekend a popular crag can sport legions of climbers and topropes every three feet, producing a kind of casual Barnum and Bailey ambience. Belayers, jostling hip to hip, spew lies back and forth and even share lunch while on the job. It is easy to forget where you are and a learned reflex (such as never removing one's brake hand from the belay rope) can become a liability instead of a protection mechanism—as "R.U.H." (Relatively Unknown Hacker) discovered while "on belay" at Taylor's Falls, Minnesota.

It was mid-September and the crag was crowded as a Timberwolve's game. The humidity had the rock "slicker than deer guts on a doorknob." Even the falls seemed to radiate heat and sweat. R.U.H. was belaying "No-Pro Bill." No-Pro Bill had earned his title through his ineptness at placing even the most straightforward gear, and his awful practice of simply pushing on without it. Presently, however, No-Pro was forty feet up on a toprope manned by R.U.H., who was adrift in thought, pole-axed by heat and humidity, complacent in the crowd.

What began as a prickling sensation about his back and legs quickly swelled into the stabbing pain of 10,000 arrow wounds—hornets! The whole clan of stingers as well as some relatives from across the river were at it now. Not his first run-in with these vile bugs, R.U.H. had a well-developed coping mechanism: running!

Since he was unanchored, a mere twist of his locking biner on the front of his harness was all it took to unleash R.U.H. from his belay of No-Pro Bill, whence he stampeded over several thousand adjacent craggers and dove headfirst into the nearby creek. Although No-Pro was

BzzHAWzz z
Bz HAWzz
BBzHAWHAWzz
HAWzz z z

SPLASH

accustomed to climbing well above his protection, the sight of an empty-handed ATC dangling from his rope so very far below set him shaking like Hiawatha facing the Black Bear. The crux was a done thing, however, and No-Pro played the psychology of "easier ground" to the hilt while someone scrambled to re-establish the belay.

COMMENTARY: R.U.H. panicked and forsook an obligation so sacred and conspicuous that it goes without saying: come hornets or high water, the belayer *never* abandons the cord. At the very least R.U.H. could have flipped No-Pro the belay strand of the doubled rope so he, No-Pro, could hold himself on (or try to) till someone else could grab the line. This is a dangerous option but better than simply unclipping and dashing off—which is grounds for cruel and unusual punishment to be levied against R.U.H., no matter what the size and seriousness of his many stinger welts.

PREVENTION: Shagging a belay from anyone with a belay device and a few spare minutes is risky business. Use common sense in choosing your belayer, for they literally have your life in their hands.

# 4

# THE DEVIL VISITS ANGEL FALLS

*Californians nearly washed into Next World*

Jim and Stu, two California big-wall masters, ventured to the other-worldly Venezuelan rain forest intent on pushing a direct route up the overhanging, chilling and mist-swept wall left of spectacular Salto Angel (Angel Falls), the largest falls on earth (3,312 feet). First, the long flight to South America, then another hop in a puddle-jumper to the remote resort/dump known as Canaima, deep in primordial jungle. A wild, two-day trip via motorized canoe brought the climbers to an open-air bush camp half a mile from the falls. The boatman/guide would remain at the camp for the duration of Jim and Stu's climb, then would ferry the pair back to Canaima.

Now during early December, the legendary gusher was but a soft silver ribbon. Owing to the decreased flow, the duo had climbing options that nine months out of the year were either partially or totally underwater. The most stunning line was an aid crack rifling straight off the boulder-strewn base and soaring, unbroken, for nearly 3,000 feet, passing through several large roofs before melding into a latticework of wide cracks and corners over the last few hundred feet to the rim. This, by far, was *the* line on the intimidating wall, which overhung some ten degrees for the first several thousand feet. Jim and Stu licked their chops over what was obviously an aid route for the ages, a route they fixed two pitches on the very afternoon they arrived. Though the insects were fiendish and the expansive rain forest spooky and brooding, the sky was cloudless and sapphire blue, so the next day the duo cast off with high hopes of completing the route in seven days, barring unseen hitches. Over the first two days the pair made good time up the uniform crack, dusting off twelve pitches, every inch aid ranging from A1 to a little A3 on the tenth lead. They made it perhaps halfway up the great wall, and judging by their progress thus far, they reckoned to top out a couple days early if the looming overhangs didn't require too many shenanigans. However, that night it began to rain. Protected by the overhanging wall, they dangled in their portaledges and watched "raindrops the size of walnuts" whistle through the air some ways out in open space. The next morning, the rain had increased to a deluge, the falls had swollen to ten times its previous size and the boys were getting pummeled by the spray. The updrafts were so vicious they whipped the ropes out into space and at times partially unweighted the haulbag from the anchors. The gusher, growing by the minute, flashed past them in a solid shaft only fifty feet to their right. This was the "dry" season, but the jungle apparently didn't know as much. As if climbing underneath water cannons trained on his torso, Stu tried to pendulum left and affect some distance between the team and the swelling falls—but no go. They couldn't possibly rap off down an overhanging wall in the blasting monsoon. That left one choice: nail like maniacs toward the first giant roof some 200 feet overhead, and hope to get some shelter from the gusher. Jim racked up every peg they had and frantically bashed up the A2 crack to another sling belay, the fourteenth one in a row. By the time Stu had gained the belay (he left half the pegs behind, unable to remove them), the falls were torpedoing by him only twenty feet away, and a six-inch sheet of water was streaming down the face, splashing off every bump and rib and nearly drowning the Californians.

Jim cast off on the next lead, reaching into the torrent to place pins, bashing his fingers trying to hammer though the stream and drive home the pegs. It took him nearly two hours to nail fifty feet to the roof which, luckily, described a pronounced, arcing crown, the right (falls) side of which curved twenty feet down to form a sheltered grotto. Out of the water at last, Jim rigged a bomber anchor and tied off. By the time Stu reached the belay, the left edge of the falls was cascading over the lip of the roof "like a continuous wave breaking out in space behind us." Stu likened their mind-boggling position to "being holed up in an upside-down little patio with a stone awning overhead." With the gusher falling ten feet away, the pair were protected from the wind, and the arc of the overhang kept the lateral spray off them as well. They set up their portaledges and stared out into space at perhaps what no other climbers had ever witnessed on a wall: a seamless curtain of water—a view from behind the great falls—rushing past them, so close they could almost reach out and touch it. By late afternoon the curtain was "perhaps twenty feet thick" and extended over the entire width of the overhang under which, for the time being, the Californians were trapped.

The "time being" turned into three days in what Stu described as a sort of roaring hallucination, "entombed in this little hollow and locked there by a vertical ocean streaming past our very faces." Early the third day the weather cleared, evidenced by the blinding rainbows and light play of the sun on the crystalline sheet falling before them. Three more days passed before the falls finally receded and the Californians again had an open view to the world. Now out of food, and astonished to be alive, the pair spent day seven rapping off, an epic in its own right involving down-nailing and wild swings necessary to get into the overhanging wall and rig the next anchors. If this wasn't suffering enough, the boatman/guide had given the Gringos up for dead and headed back to Canaima. With no trail to beat it back to the resort, the pair could only hunker down and wait for the next load of tourists to come calling. They waited nearly a week, living off wild berries for the last three days.

COMMENTARY: I've heard of rainstorms in the Dolomites sending torrents down large dihedrals, causing all kinds of mischief for climbers stranded there. But experiencing such a torrent (to say nothing of the world's largest waterfall) from the backside, while dangling in relative safety, is surely a unique experience.

PREVENTION: Climbing in equatorial regions cannot be compared to climbing in temperate zones. Wild swings in weather are the norm. Weather forecasts are lacking. In my experience, which includes more than twenty trips into jungled areas, the best policy is to expect the worst, because if you're there for more than a week, you're likely to get it. It's for good reason they call it a "rain forest."

# 5

# RABBI GUNTHER SAYS 'ENOUGH'

*He surely fudged on his Kosher diet*

"Brother" Bob, Ziggy and I were conducting a beginning climbing class for a dozen young adults (13–17 years old), members of an excruciatingly conservative Los Angeles synagogue. The Youth Outing Club, as the group was known, was headed up by one Rabbi Buddy, a strapping ex-Israeli Army Ranger who took his adventure sports as seriously as he did the Torah, and the measureless Rabbi Gunther, who stood 5'2" in boots and went at about 450 pounds. So far as I understood, the considerable Rabbi Gunther was there to ensure the religious integrity of the group; Brother Bob, however, suggested that Rabbi Buddy used the Youth Outing Club as a ploy to escape the severity of the synagogue to go scuba diving, parachuting, skiing, climbing and so forth. If so, Rabbi Buddy had with him a dozen kindred spirits on this blistering morn at Joshua Tree, where we had strung a series of topropes on a mid-angled slab. The young boys, stripped down to gym trunks and rock shoes owing to blast-furnace desert heat, scampered up the slab faster than Lazarus bolted from his sarcophagus. The six girls—owing to custom (conceived and enforced by old men) decreeing that all female flesh must be covered—were swathed like mummies and tended to climb slower, stopping every other move to gasp and fan themselves. Off to the side, stationed in the meager shade of a Joshua Tree, the momentous Rabbi Gunther rocked back and forth, reading from a holy book the size of a playing card and muttering in a strange tongue to no one in particular. The great Rabbi's plaintive dirge; the stark desert sky; the young faithful, half of them seminude, the other half swaddled head to toe; the feisty Rabbi Buddy, now climbing, now barking orders, now laughing, now thanking Yahweh that he should bequeath us these rocks; and the three of us climbing bums, trying to keep a lid on things. All told, the milieu was a peculiar one, even by crag standards—but the strangeness of the scene went up ten notches when the extensive Rabbi Gunther trousered his text, cleared his throat like Moses before delivering the Commandments, and declared himself ready to climb. His formidable girth presented problems so far as getting him tied into the cord. Eventually we managed to lash together four or five old twenty-foot swami belts of two-inch webbing and fashion the copious Rabbi a crude if workable (we hoped) sit sling. Brother Bob went to the top of the slab and beefed up the anchor with an additional twenty or thirty nuts, pitons, and camming devices. Ziggy rigged a ground directional (to belay through) by way of a long sling girth hitched round the base of a titanic barrel cactus growing some ways back from the slab. Should the spacious Rabbi somehow surmount the slab, which we couldn't imagine, he'd have to be lowered off. Without the directional, the moment the bounteous Rabbi leaned back on the line Ziggy would be hurled halfway to the West Bank. About this time Rabbi Buddy pulled me aside and said, "Look, we gotta somehow get this guy up the slab or my program could get scrapped." We agreed I would solo alongside the commodious Rabbi, pointing out every hand and foot placement. More we could not do. Indeed, all the Pharisees were not strong enough to hoist the abundant Rabbi up the slab.

CLOSE CALLS

Rabbi Gunther rubbed his hands together fast enough to start a fire. Then he set his jaw and started up. Astonishingly, the plentiful Rabbi was light on his feet, though I was just waiting for the grommets to blow out of his rock shoes or for the stitching to suddenly give way. Faster than I could point out the holds the ample Rabbi was on them, moving smoothly now, up to midslab, and showing poise and balance I never would have suspected—when suddenly he said, "That's enough," and immediately leaned back, pushing off the slab, he shock-loaded onto the rope.

The cord twanged tight. The anchors creaked like the rigging on a tug boat. Ziggy locked off his load whence the directional anchor sling snugged tight and pinched off the giant cactus like a radish, and the next thing we knew Ziggy was bounding across the tundra like a man dragged behind a stallion. Somehow Ziggy's bounding carcass provided enough counterweight and the vast Rabbi deftly stepped to the ground just as Ziggy was dashed into the cliffside.

COMMENTARY: It took Ziggy several hours to pick the gravel and quills from his hide. If this wasn't indignity enough, a park ranger soon arrived on the scene and issued Zig a citation for destroying deciduous matter within national park boundaries—which is a federal offense. (A fine which Rabbi Buddy paid, pleased as he was that the far-reaching Rabbi Gunther had made time on the slab and that his program was still a go.) Extricating the portly Rabbi from his rigging was problematic, however. The rotund Rabbi's tie-in knot had cinched down to the size of a pea. All efforts to untie it—including half an hour with a rigging tool—were fruitless, and Brother Bob eventually had to cut the rope. Another half hour of wiggling, yanking and cursing were sufficient to loosen the water knot on the bulbous Rabbi's make-shift sit harness.

PREVENTION: We've all gone overweight at some time, though few of us have put on an additional 200 pounds. Fewer still have put on such imposing tallow and ended up at the crags.

Had we done so, our appearance would have demanded special attention. All jokes aside, we should have been square with the swollen Rabbi, said that we feared the system needed to be revised to accommodate his substantial person, and arranged to belay him off twin ropes. I've never seen this idea put into practice, but it would have eliminated the great disparity in weight between Ziggy and the inflated Rabbi, thus making the situation manageable.

# 6

# MADNESS ON THE SPIRE

*Under the knife on Lost Arrow*

Seattle climbers Russell and Billy set their sights on the Lost Arrow Spire, a semi-detached pinnacle right of Upper Yosemite Falls, but several years passed before the team found themselves in Yosemite Valley, ready to tackle the "flint hard and flawless" bullet of gray and orange granite, arguably America's most famous summit. The pair would follow standard procedure: trudge up the Yosemite Falls trail to the north rim, rappel 180 feet into the notch separating the spire from the main wall, grapple up the spire, and return to the rim via Tyrolean traverse.

On the rim, Russell tied two ropes together and secured one end to a stout pine set back from the brink, directly above the notch. He chucked the other end into the notch below. With a third rope coiled around his shoulder, Russell rappelled into the notch and Billy followed. The team would lead on the third rope, with Russell trailing the ropes that were tied together and secured to the pine.

Billy tied in and tiptoed out on a small ledge to the start of the climbing, 2,000 feet of mountain air plunging beneath his heels. Four hours later, Russell frictioned up the final step of this fabulous stone satellite and joined Billy on the summit. Billy, an excitable young man of twenty-five birthdays, broke into tears; but in five minutes, his mood would sour appreciably. Russell, 45, stoic and dry as Methuselah's bones, pulled up the slack on the trail rope till it ran taut from their bolt anchor atop the spire, stretched across sixty feet of void and over to the pine tree on the north rim.

By now several suspicious-looking young men had approached the pine tree on the rim. One began exploring the rope and rigging, whereupon the combustible Billy screamed that if the stranger so much as touched the line, he would rip the stranger's heart out with his bare hands. The stranger inquired how Billy planned to do that from the top of the spire. Billy shrieked and blustered till the veins in his neck looked like crimped hoses.

The stranger listened patiently; then, with an upward

IF YOU SO MUCH AS LOOK AT THAT ROPE I'LL TEAR OUT YER HEART, LUNGS, KIDNEYS, SPLEEN & GIZZARD TOO...

flick of a pocketknife, severed the rope from the pine. If this was not punishment enough, the two strangers began pelting Billy and Russell with stones, transforming Billy into a regular Mr. Hyde. It was all Russell could do to restrain him.

Eventually the strangers wandered off, laughing. Billy and Russell, sorely welted from the stoning and stranded on the exposed summit, were able to attract the attention of other hikers, who reported the two's predicament to the rangers. Billy and Russell endured a chilly bivouac on the lonely steeple. The following morning, YOSAR rangers arrived and fired a new line across the gap via a rope gun. Billy and Russell were able to affect their airy Tyrolean escape to solid ground.

COMMENTARY: This is not the first time, nor will it be the last, that hikers have tinkered with fixed lines. Often it's impossible to know what has occurred: has some imbecile fiddled with the biners, untied the knots, or what?

PREVENTION: Leave a small, handwritten note stating that climbers' lives depend on the ropes remaining undisturbed. That is usually enough to dissuade even the most cold-hearted hiker from becoming party to homicide by tampering with the precious lines. In Russell and Billy's case, they would likely have been fine until Billy opened his pie hole and began spewing hollow threats. A simple explanation of the gravity of the situation should have been enough.

# 7
# LOVE ON
# THE CLIFFSIDE

*Love strikes twice on infamous Yosemite outing*

Sam was a Yosemite regular long after poverty had driven other Valley veterans into the real world of car payments and domestic anguish. Consequently, Sam often found himself with empty pockets and burning loins. Then he met Misty in Yosemite's popular Mountain Room bar one night, and over the span of a dozen beers, he hatched a reckless plan: take the comely Misty up the *South Face* of Washington Column.

Having presented himself as one of Yosemite's finest—a patent untruth—Sam convinced the gullible Misty that she'd be in capable hands. Misty, a self-described physical-education student and aerobics instructor from Clovis, California, sported a hale and toned corpus, so Sam figured she was equal to the task of jumaring up the menacing 1,600-foot wall.

Until Sam racked up at the base of the great climb the following morning, Misty had never before seen a kernmantle rope. Sam briefly explained the basics and flew up the first lead. Astonishingly, Misty followed on the jugs without pause, taking to the job handily. By early afternoon the pair had gained Dinner Ledge, where the turgid Sam had planned to have a fine time of it. But on the ledge they discovered a party of seven Japanese climbers already camped. The ledge was spacious, but lacked privacy. Sam changed plans and cast off on the pitches above, gaining the easy exit cracks an hour before nightfall. As a precaution, Sam had packed two hammocks, and in the absence of a suitable ledge, rigged said hammocks to the cliff, one hanging atop the other.

According to Sam, Misty showed no concern at being lashed to the side of a sheer rock wall, over a quarter mile above the talus. Following a meal of gorp, cheese, and red table wine, Sam wooed Misty into his lower hammock. Sam quickly found that the harnesses limited their options; so he painstakingly rigged two hangman's nooses,

fitted them snugly around their respective ankles, and they performed the wild thing for many glorious hours (which included several improbable postures he had seen in a book from Hyderabad, India).

Thus sated, Sam assisted Misty into the higher hammock and got her tied back in taut to the anchor. Standing in his own hammock to accomplish this task, Sam suddenly heard a rueful rip down by his feet—and then found himself plunging as if falling through a trap door. He was jerked to a stop some dozen feet below, upside down, his entire life suspended solely by the rope noosed round his ankle. The shadow-like forms floating down to the ground were nothing but his own clothes.

Sam frantically clawed up his own leg, clasped the rope, and batmanned up to his tattered hammock. Fumbling in the dark, he managed to get harnessed back up and tied in. He used the remains of his hammock as a breechcloth, and the pair topped out early the next day.

COMMENTARY: It is said that scrotal coals will drive a man to the end of the galaxy, but I wonder if Buck Rogers himself ever went farther than Sam did that infamous night on Washington Column.

PREVENTION: This escapade is a fantastic story, but it sends a lethal message to aspiring big-wall climbers. By any measure this whole business was madness. A big wall—even the most traveled wall in the world—is no place to break in a beginner. What's amazing is that with all the complicated rigging and techniques involved, Sam didn't botch a clip or a rope transfer and get them both killed.

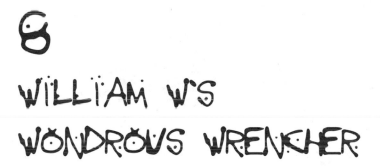

# 8

# WILLIAM W'S WONDROUS WRENCHER

*Willoughby wheezed, whimpered, and whistled off*

William Willoughby and the winsome woman Wendy Winkle were walking west alongside the water-streaked Winston Wall in Washington. Struck by the stunning steepness of *Sisyphus,* which showcased seventy feet of severe stemming (5.10), they strode through shrubs to the sheer stone, and Willoughby, now shod and stoked, started stemming seriously. Willoughby cruised till his calves cramped after a couple cubits of continuous contortions—but he casually cranked the crux, though for his concrete calves and consumed corpus he couldn't clip a fixed Camelot crammed in the corner of the curving and complex crack.

Willoughby now wobbled well above a woeful Walnut, whimpering to Wendy Winkle to watch him. Willoughby wheezed, wept, and whistled off, twice whacking the wall on his way toward the winsome Wendy Winkle, who locked off the leader like a load of lumber. Willoughby dangled like a dead dog from his dreadful drop, having stopped seven short spans from soil.

COMMENTARY: Another example of someone skipping protection and "going for it" without having any "it" to go for— except a gigantic fall.

EARTH
5636891142 mi.

FRIENDLY MANITOBA

PREVENTION: Committing to an unprotected crux when pumped is a perilous tactic. Unless you have experience climbing pumped, and well know your abilities when the gas is gone, it's much safer to back down rather than hoping you can pull off something miraculous. This is not so much a concern on clip & go sport routes, providing one doesn't skip clips; in fact, it's on well-protected routes where one can learn how to climb through—or at any rate, climb with— a massive pump. Unprotected rock is no place to discover how well (or how poorly) you can perform when the body has no more.

# 9

# MEXICAN INDULGENCE

*Why do you think they call it dope?*

Todd and Paul, both hailing from San Diego, California, were sick of the slabs at Tahquitz and Suicide and anxious to set their teeth into something *mas dificil y mas grande*. Their eyes naturally turned south of the border, toward El Gran Trono Blanco—The Great White Throne—a shocking, 1,600-foot fist of Caucasian granite rearing off the lonesome grit of Laguna Salada wilderness, some five hours drive into Baja, Mexico.

Their goal was the 5.10c grade V on the Throne's shady south face, a trade route notorious for its "La Fiesta" ledge at midheight, the standard bivouac and locale of untold debaucheries. They survived the drive in, over dirt roads prowled by range curs and highwaymen. Early the next morning the team began the bitter trudge to the cliff and roped up around noon—ample time to dust off the eight pitches to La Fiesta ledge. There they would consume quantities of mescal Todd had purchased in Mexicali and would huff some of the herb Todd had also hauled along. Then both would gaze like perfect morons into the Latin sky.

The first pitches (5.8–5.10) passed swimmingly. Both climbers were fluent in slab duty. Todd led off on the eighth and final pitch before La Fiesta. Paul belayed. Todd polished off sketchy moves up a leaning ramp, clipped a fixed wire, and traversed dead left some thirty feet to a rounded groove leading to the famous ledge. In minutes, Todd had anchored off. Presently the haul line came snug. Paul unclipped the haulbag from the anchor and cut it loose. The bag described a steep arc, bounding across the face before coming to a stop in the plumbline beneath Todd's anchor.

Only when Paul had jugged up to the ledge and got set to dig into the bag for the intoxicants did he discover that most of the lead rack—which had been clipped to the top of the bag—was missing. Apparently, it had come unclipped from the haulbag when it had been cut loose and careened across the wall. Todd was furious; Paul was ashamed. They could not proceed up the wall without the missing gear, and it was too late to descend. They bitterly kicked back on the ledge, drank their liquor, and smoked their herb.

The next morning, dehydrated from the vile mescal, they discovered that in the brief but costly flight of the haulbag the previous day, both of their two remaining water bottles had sprung leaks and were now dry. Not a drop. They rappelled off the wall, retrieved the scattered gear, and bolted back to the car. Their thirst was getting critical. They found a half-empty bottle of warm Coke in the back seat, and this revived them somewhat. But Todd's car—a sad Rambler with 300,000 miles—wouldn't start. Dead battery.

The duo exhausted themselves trying to push-start the heap through ankle-deep sand; it finally kicked over about three that afternoon and then started puttering toward the main road. By this time both men were half dead with thirst. Paul's tongue had swelled to the size of a summer sausage. Then late that afternoon, only six miles from the road, they got a flat. Todd was hallucinating while he changed the tire. Darkness fell and the two cragsmen passed out in the Rambler. They started out at dawn the following day, as withered as baked apples. Then the Rambler got stuck in a dune within sight of the road, and Todd swears that he and Paul would still be there, bleached bones in the old Rambler, had it not been for the munificence of a peon with a mule cart who dragged them onto the tarmac.

After trying to rehydrate at a local *bodega*, the duo putted back to San Diego via San Ysidro, where Paul actually spent several hours in the hospital while nurses pumped his shriveled carcass full with IVs.

COMMENTARY: These climbers were woefully unprepared for their Latin adventure. A long, remote climb should always be approached as serious business. This debacle illustrates the consequences when climbers are not focused on safety.

PREVENTION: Travel to wilderness areas with at least two cars if your team is likely to be alone. Always take more food and water than you think you'll need; leave a good amount in the car for after the climb. Lastly, a haulbag should never be cut loose to swing and bound across the rock. Often a loop of slack in either the lead or trail rope can be used to lower out the bag. Otherwise, a length of lightweight cord will suffice.

# 10

# MAD WAVES AND ENGLISHMEN

*Taking the royal bath*

Two Englishmen, Winston and Charles, drove their Jaguar sedan to the chilling, sea-swept cliffs of Soccershire, near Land's End on the southwestern coast. Sorely hungover, the mates stopped at a cafe for beans and bangers, then drove to the seashore and spent several more hours chain-smoking, sorting pegs and crabs, and applying several Troy gallons of sunblock to their pallid torsos, after which they absailed several hundred feet to a small ledge cutting across the disgusting, chalky cliffside.

Fifteen feet below, swollen combers slammed against the wall sending roostertails of spume over the Englishmen. "Bloody hell!" Winston wailed, soaked to the bone. "We've f@#$ing got to find a f$%@ing belay and get the f$&k out of here!" Charles shuffled left till the ledge ran out on the blank cliff where he slung a Wilkenson Sword with a long runner and rigged a sling belay, the hungry waves lapping at his plimsoles. Winston hiked up his knickers, blew his nose on his cravat and traversed to the sling belay; then he started up a steep wall resplendent with splendid knobs.

After twenty feet, Winston slung a particularly splendid knob, broke wind, and pushed on. Ten more feet out, he highstepped a carbuncle smeared with birdlime. With no handholds to speak of or crank off, Winston started pressing his leg straight, six inches, then a foot when . . . PING! His foot blew off.

"Bollocks!"

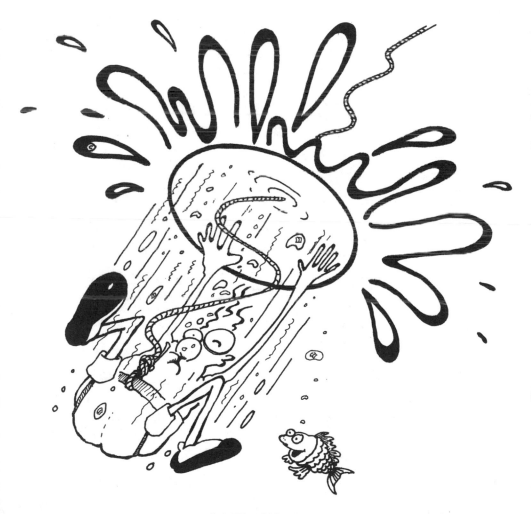

He pitched down the chalky cliffside, impacting the sling on the horn and wrenching Charles up an Imperial yard, thus lifting Charles's belay sling off the Wilkenson Sword, whence he dropped down. Now both Englishmen dangled from the runner draped over the splendid knob above.

Ping!

SPLASH!

COMMENTARY: Luckily, Charles was a strong swimmer and, half hauling the waterlogged and panicked Winston, managed to swim them both to a rock shelf where they could scramble out of the drink and, several hours later, clamber up to freedom.

PREVENTION: All belay anchors must be multi-directional to avoid the Englishmen's fate. Simply slinging a jive, crumbling spike of sea-cliff choss and casting off is not a bold move, but a reckless one.

# 11

# AFFAIR OF THE MALEVOLENT "CHAMBERPOT"

*Tallywhacker sliced to the quick in the High Cascades*

Four experienced mountaineers set out from Seattle to scale the lofty *West Ridge* of Eldorado Peak in the North Cascades, Washington. The quartet slogged to a height of about 6,645 feet before cruel winds and gusting snow forced them to bivouac. Clothed more for a summer outing than an alpine epic, the team's provisions consisted mainly of 24-ounce cans of Foster's Lager. It was said of the oldest team member (call him "Peter") that beer passed through him like water passes through a duck. Owing to this disposition, Peter usually carried a plastic, zip-locked bag for emergencies. If you consider a plastic bag an improbable chamberpot, and Peter something less than a genius for choosing same, read on . . . .

As it happens, Peter forgot his plastic bag on this trip and had to make do with an empty can of Foster's Lager. According to Peter, during one of his "nocturnal wakenings, high winds and snow made impeccable maneuvering difficult." I'm not sure why the snow affected Peter's aim, but in the process of whizzing into the can Peter managed to tragically lacerate the very quick of his tallywhacker.

Never mind frostbite or cerebral edema, this was a true medical emergency. Peter performed a "firm squeeze" technique to staunch the blood flow till the first aid kit could be looted for steri-strips which were "quickly applied longitudinally." Closure was affected, and with "no further trauma or change in morphology," a descent was completed the following morning. (Source: Accidents in North American Mountaineering, 1989)

COMMENTARY: This epic brings to light a topic that all climbers face on multiday routes, but of which few people ever speak: what is the best way to relieve yourself on a long climb? I can state from experience that trade routes on El Capitan—as well as many other popular big walls—have at times been reduced to vertical latrines. Certain ledges have gotten so toxic and nauseating that climbers sometimes stop short of or climb past these ledges and bivouac in aid slings, rather than spend the night gagging on urine and feces fumes. For waste management, most wall climbers have opted to go with wide-mouth PVC "tubes" (four-inch diameter with secure, screw-on lids) that serve as portable toilets, the contents being hauled off for proper disposal. "Letting it fly" is no longer an acceptable practice, even on wilderness walls. The Park Service and other land-managing agencies are requiring the use of tubes in several areas—good thing, too, as a classic wall can be turned into a literal shit house without their use.

PREVENTION: So far as physical hazards go, the male climber is well served to keep his private equipment far away from sharp metal objects. The female climber knows this already.

# 12.

# RESCUE TEAM TACKLES THE FALLS

*Just who sold that man a knife?!*

A regional search and rescue team were practicing at a local, seventy-foot high waterfall. A "victim" and "rescuer" were shivering in the drink at the base of the cascade. The duo had tied themselves to a "hauling" line and a "belay" line that had been dropped from the top of the

falls, where a "rescue" team commenced with a "vertical raising," intending to pull the drenched pair up to "safety."

The duo had been hauled to a height of about twenty-five feet when the prusik knot on the haul line clenched onto the rope like wolverine jaws. The rigging got entangled and, in short, the "rescuer" panicked and proceeded to execute a maneuver more preposterous than any I've ever done (which is really saying something). Pulling out a hunting knife and wielding it like a crazed butcher, the "rescuer" freed his "victims" by slashing the rope in twain. The duo instantly plunged down the falls and splashed in. The dazed pair were quickly drawn into fierce rapids and swept about sixty yards downstream till they finally hove to on the "belay" line, whence they clawed onto a rock, where tourists then pulled the pair—peppered with contusions—to safety.

The business of cutting the rope can be written off to panic, but who was watching the "belay" rope? Said "belayer" paid out roughly 200 feet of line before arresting the pair downstream! Judging by the details of this "rescue," it's a wonder that the entire "rescue team" didn't end up in the drink.

PREVENTION: In such popular climbing areas as Yosemite, Rocky Mountain National Park, the Grand Tetons, etc., rescue teams are typically made up of experts with years of hands-on experience. Conversely, small-time regional rescue teams sometimes feature good 'ol boys more steeped in bear hunting, strip poker and Monday Night Football than in the rudiments of mountaineering. A vertical raising is a complicated and gear-intensive procedure that can confound professionals and spank amateurs like there's no tomorrow. This incident is good reason to make every possible bid to execute a self-rescue unless injuries or circumstances absolutely rule it out. (Source: Accidents in North American Mountaineering, 1992)

# 13

# LIGHTS ALMOST OUT ON INSOMNIA

*Acapulco Dave dives again*

Throughout the early 70s, the southern California climbing community was full of celebrated characters, none more so than Acapulco Dave. It was strictly false that Dave had no brains at all, as many maintained; however it was well established that Dave had fifty parts of daring for one part of wit.

In any case, Dave earned his moniker through chronic attempts to scale the steepest, grimmest cracks of the era. He would pant and claw to within inches of the top, where on untold occasions he'd run out of gas and take electrifying, headfirst screamers, assuming in midflight the classic, layout positioning of the acclaimed cliffdivers in Acapulco. For sheer length and overall majesty, Dave's dives were equal to the Mexicans, though he tended to lose form after forty or fifty feet. So it was in the spring of 1973 when this legendary character started up *Insomnia Crack* (Suicide Rock, southern California), an overhanging gash renowned for greasy, insecure, rattling, bogus, uncertain off-finger jams. Acapulco Dave had barely slotted the first nut when a huge crowd swarmed about the base of *Insomnia* like paparazzi at the premier of Titanic; they knew they were in for a stellar showing.

About fifty feet up, Dave copped a rest at a foothold inside a flare. Just above, he'd have to yard his carcass out of the pod via rattling finger jams— but not before acquaintances on the deck demanded Dave slot no less than six nuts to protect the dire whistler they were confident he was in for.

The pro now set, Dave cast off, torquing his way up the crack. He quickly jammed past the crux (5.11c) and reached a point where the jams widened slightly but curved left across an overhanging, 100-degree wall. Dave's quaking limbs and typhoon breathing made it clear he was working on dwindling steam. Feeling he could either skip placing much-needed pro and jam for the top (another fifteen feet), or place a nut and fall off, Dave, not surprisingly, chose the former tactic. This proved a vastly poor decision, for after wobbling and huffing an additional ten feet he suddenly screamed, "I'm off!"

Nigh twenty-five feet above his last nut, Acapulco Dave dove off the cliff and described a graceful head-first trajectory. Grazing the edge of the flare, he plummeted like a rag-doll another twenty feet before wrenching to a stop some five feet off the deck. His many fans gathered round to congratulate Acapulco Dave for providing such a splendid show—and also to inspect his wounds. However, many rubberneckers were dismayed that Dave had not scratch one. They realized that the experience would pass through his mind like clouds through an empty sky, and that they would be the ones who, in the still of the night, would bolt upright in the sack with images of Acapulco Dave plunging for the Promised Land.

COMMENTARY: Another example of someone getting so pumped they cannot place protection, and choosing to carry on without it. The question here is: is there ever an instance where this tactic is even remotely sane? The answer depends on the specifics of a given route, and the degree of risk a climber considers acceptable. There isn't an experienced climber out there who hasn't had to go for it at some time. The question is, what is "it?" If, for example, Jasper is forty feet up a 100-foot thin crack, so pumped he can't stop to slot a nut, and he chooses to go for it, clearly he's "going" for nothing short of a gigantic fall. If, on the other hand, there's a rest hold a body length above and Jasper is only ten feet or so above his last piece, he might be justified in trying to go for it if he's willing to take the fall and said fall appears harmless (meaning the last piece of pro is bomber and there's nothing to hit when he pings off). If there is no rest hold till the anchor sixty feet above, Jasper is out of his mind, because he will essentially be soloing the rest of the climb.

PREVENTION: Skipping protection and "going for it" is a judgment call and should only be considered by climbers who have enough experience to take a calculated risk. Generally speaking, if a climber has to forego protection to keep climbing, he better have something pretty good to go for, and that something better be pretty close since the climber's fatigue is only going to increase the higher he goes. Other scenarios in this book present different shades of the thorny issue of "going for it." It's something that has to be taken on a case by case basis, but as a general rule climbing out of control is not the wisest option.

# 14

# ASS-DRAGGED IN WISCONSIN

*The Devil (in the lake) made him do it.*

Ronnie and a host of friends and relatives had escaped the torpid confines of the cheese factory where they worked and had ventured to Devils Lake, Wisconsin, for an afternoon of toproping on a high-angle slab peppered with quartzite knobs. An adept cragsman, Ronnie was breaking down the toprope anchors when his sister, Penelope, shouted up for him to drop the line so she could pump a final lap up the classic *Cyclops's Crack*—before returning to the cheese factory.

Ronnie guffawed, but agreed—despite the fact that he'd already cleaned and lowered most of his gear. He noticed an "ancient, albeit bomber" ring bolt above *Cyclops's Crack*, and he still had with him a long runner of one-inch tubular nylon webbing ("tube"). So he anchored off to the ancient, albeit bomber ring bolt with the runner, and belayed Penelope off his harness.

Penelope quickly dispatched the pitch and Ronnie lowered her back to the surface of the earth. Just as she touched down her husband, Ulysses, requested Ronnie belay him up *Lotus Eater*, a seditious thin crack. Ronnie didn't fancy the belay setup, as *Lotus Eater* was some dozen feet off to the side of his ancient, albeit bomber ring-bolt anchor. To protect Ulysses from an epic pendulum (should he fall), Ronnie would either have to return to the deck and fetch more gear—to rig another anchor in line with *Lotus Eater*—or extend his runner cum tie-in so he could sit directly above *Lotus Eater*, twelve feet to the side of the ancient, albeit bomber ring bolt. Since Ulysses was an intrepid 5.11 climber, Ronnie decided on the latter, riskier belay setup.

Sitting comfortably on the flat top of the cliff, some ten feet back from the lip, Ronnie shouted down that Ulysses was "on." Ulysses started up *Lotus Eater*, trying to outrun the sunset. After seventeen moves, as shadows danced up the stone wall, Ulysses found himself in an Odyssey of slippery jams and borderline layaways. Then he went and got his hands crossed—and flew off.

Completely without warning, Ronnie was yanked toward the 90-degree edge of the cliff—and kept skidding "halfway to Ithaca." Ronnie dug in his heels and leaned back as his ass was being sliced to head-cheese by spiked quartzite warts. "I pushed as hard as I could with my heels on the glass face below," Ronnie commented. "I swear there were nymphs holding the bottoms of my feet. As I screamed

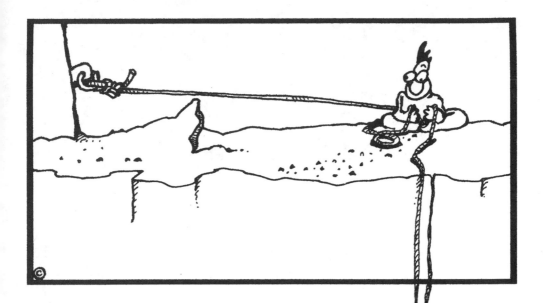

at Ulysses to get back on the route, I glanced sideways at the blade of rock over which my anchoring webbing was going to slice in two when I slid off, sending Ulysses and me to Mount Olympus to join our forefathers. But through the grace of the gods, Ulysses got back onto the route and I didn't slide off."

COMMENTARY: There's a simple saying that applies to all situations like the one in which Ronnie found himself: when you are belaying a second up a pitch, and the anchor is behind you, and you are not situated in the direct line of pull, and the climber below comes off—you will be dragged into the line of pull. Better to situate yourself in the line of pull to begin with and avoid getting "ass-dragged." Though we might chuckle at Ronnie's misfortune, the situation can be fatal if the belayer starts twirling, hits a limb or his head, and somehow loses control of the belay.

PREVENTION: Simple: when you are belaying a second up a pitch, and the anchor is behind you, always get in the direct line of pull, with no slack in the rope between your harness and the anchor point.

# 15

# TOOTH AND NAIL IN ARCO

*Hal chews the cord*

Dirk, a young American, was fresh out of college. Through a hot tip from his climbing partner, Hal, Dirk managed to land a dream job in Europe, where he pulled down sufficient ducats to squander his free time traveling, drinking, wenching and climbing—apparently in that order. Six months into his dream gig, Hal and his girlfriend Frida joined Dirk in Europe for a "grand tour." Hal snagged his friends at the airport in a big BMW, and the trio set off. Their grand tour got hung up in Kreuzberg, however, where the bars never close and where Dirk and Hal consumed vast quantities of beer for two days straight as Frida slept off her jet lag in the back seat of the Beemer.

Altogether besotted, the two boys roused Frida and set off for Arco, a now-familiar spot for Dirk. The boys still had a load on when they headed up *The Maiden*, a classic, ten-pitch 5.10 testpiece. Adventurous as he was, Hal was never comfortable leading anything beyond 5.9, so Dirk took the sharp end exclusively. Still stunned by their forty-eight-hour binge, the pair moved slowly over the first few leads as "little Italian monkey teenagers climbed all over us, using our heads as footholds."

At noon, the duo hove to at the crux eighth lead. The booze had worn off and both climbers were feeling woozy and dry as a Jane Austen novel. Dirk cast off. The climbing was difficult, bulgy face climbing with a few traverses thrown in for good measure. Dirk finally clawed onto a big belay ledge and collapsed, cursing the man who invented alcoholic beverages. Hal was out of view and communication was impossible, so Dirk simply yanked the rope tight and started belaying.

An hour passed. Suddenly the rope felt weighted and stayed that way for several minutes. Then Dirk heard some muffled groaning from far below, as though Hal was yelling up with marbles in his mouth. Then the weight came off the rope for several long seconds, after which Dirk was shock-loaded by a massive jerk that almost sawed him in half. Later, held on tension by a now-leery Dirk, Hal came pawing over the bulge and into view, utterly knackered. He gained the belay ledge and collapsed, and only later was able to relate what happened: the invention of a new "climbing" technique.

COMMENTARY: The new "technique?" It seems that poor Hal had climbed only forty or so feet when his body was overcome by a violent malaise. He proceeded to nearly puke his boots off, then began batmanning up the rope. After twenty feet the malaise returned and presently Hal's pumped guns could no longer hang onto the cord. Rather than simply let go and pitch off for a forty footer, Hal clenched the line in his teeth and began shaking out his blazing firearms. Then he had to open his mouth to upchuck again and was off for that forty footer.

PREVENTION: "A circus clown could not have dreamed up a more absurd way to follow a pitch." Or so claimed Dirk. In the final analysis, the lesson learned is that climbing requires the undivided attention of a clear mind. To be sure, a multipitch free climb at the edge of one's ability is no place to be hauling a hangover. That much said, I know very few climbers who have not climbed hungover at some time. Some climbers are always hungover. Some climb with a buzz on. It's madness, of course, and everyone knows it.

# "FORE!"

*Teeing off on El Capitan*

Throughout the 70s, Canadians Lloyd and Floyd were two of the finest and most accomplished wall climbers in the business. During a "recreational" ascent of the *Salathé Wall* on El Capitan, they hauled, in addition to three cases of Moosehead beer, a bag of 200 golf balls they'd filched off a driving range in Palm Springs. They proceeded to tee up on El Cap Tower, a flat and spacious ledge about 2,200 feet up the towering cliff. Along with the golf balls, they'd brought a three-iron, a driver and a thatch of Astro-Turf; together, they spent a pleasant June afternoon banging great drives into the meadow below.

Down in the valley, several cars were struck and windshields shattered. The rangers closed down the road for three hours and fanned out on horseback looking for a sniper. Cars backed up, overheated, rammed each other. Tourists fought. There were several arrests. As their cache of balls dwindled, their ardor rose as to who could smack the longest drive. Lloyd abandoned his fluid golf stroke (modeled after Ben Hogan, according to Lloyd) and re-verted to baseball mechanics, putting everything he had into it.

Halfway through a murderous swing, Lloyd felt something go in his back. A pang became a throb. By the next morning Lloyd could barely move his tongue for the grievous pain. Unable to jumar, the team had to bail, and even this took two days because Lloyd could only rappel in twenty-foot bursts before curling into an agonized knot.

COMMENTARY: Big wall golfing is outrageous and idiotic, and therein lies the charm—at least for our Canadian colleagues. Nevertheless, big wall golfing is not recommended. Nor is any manner of tomfoolery that could wrench one's back or divert one's attention from the serious tasks at hand.

PREVENTION: Leave the clubs in the trunk and stay focused on the climb.

# 17

# KUNG FU ON WASHINGTON COLUMN

*Ugly American gets his clock cleaned*

Two Colorado climbers, Nelson and Andy, were attempting a blitz ascent of the *South Face* of Washington Column (grade V) in Yosemite, prior to attempting a one-day ascent of the *Nose* on El Capitan. The pair started early and reached Overnight Ledge, 400 feet up the wall, by 7:30 in the morning. There they found a Taiwanese team who had bivouacked on the ledge the previous night, having fixed the two pitches above the ledge the day before. Although the Taiwanese were gearing up for the day's climbing, they suggested that Nelson and Andy carry on first because the duo was so fleet, had no bivouac gear and only one rope. Nelson and Andy agreed and set off.

All went splendidly until the exit pitches high on the wall, which follow a grungy gully. Here, when Andy was following, the lead rope jammed in a grainy groove, and two hours of fiddling and cursing could not free the line. Since Nelson and Andy carried no hammers and had no knife, there was no means with which to cut the rope and proceed on whatever remained—this the two would gladly have done if possible. As it dangled, they could either start chewing or wait for the Taiwanese team to catch up and rescue them, 100 feet from easy ground.

However, when Andy informed the Taiwanese leader that he and Nelson would need to appropriate the Taiwanese team's cord to affect their escape, the foreigner balked. Andy pressed the issue even further and a row broke out, resulting in a flurry of hatchet-like Kung Fu

moves from the Taiwanese, and a sound thrashing for the insolent American. The Taiwanese team proceeded to the top and the humbled Americans followed on the trail line, gaining the summit just as darkness fell.

COMMENTARY: Another case of bad luck and horrible diplomacy. But the fact is, if you climb long enough, your rope will at some point get stuck, and all the angels and saints in Heaven won't be able to free it.

PREVENTION: Tackling a long climb with only one rope is considered a statement on the team's prowess and moxie. If the team tops out without incident, they are "bold." If their rope gets stuck, they are fools. But how about on long wilderness routes, where a rescue is impossible? Here, if the one rope gets stuck, the team is neither bold nor foolish—they're dead. System backups keep us alive. With one rope, there is no backup, so the team has assigned the risk to themselves, regardless of their luck. So far as the Kung-Fu fighting goes, when a man is determined to be an ass, someone is bound to ride him like a donkey—and he'll have to like it. Such was the case with poor Andy.

# 18

# NELLIE'S NIGHT OUT

*Yosemite hardman learns the meaning of being "cut off"*

Longtime Yosemite hardman Nellie O. had for some weeks been working on free climbing the first six pitches of a big wall on the western flanks of El Capitan. He'd ticked off everything but a pesky tension traverse on pitch four, and on this glorious morning Nellie hoped to put that traverse to rest. His partner, the young Heather, a bubbly barmaid from the Mountain Room Broiler, had done a little toproping on Swan Slab, but otherwise had no climbing experience at all. It remains a mystery how, in a matter of moments, Nellie resolved to Heather the artful business of following a pitch on ascenders, not to mention how the svelte rookie managed the task. But she did, and in turn, Nellie managed to free climb the pesky traverse and arrive at the hanging stance atop the fourth pitch.

Nellie's mind quickly drifted into the great dihedrals high above, where he hoped to someday push the free climbing—perhaps all the way to the summit where an international reputation, and perhaps Heather, would welcome him. But not today. Heather followed the fourth pitch on jugs, and Nellie rigged the ropes to rappel, promising to talk fresh Heather through the rappel setup from the hanging stance 150 feet below. Nellie tossed the ropes into the void and started backpedaling down the cliffside, playing up the part of the dauntless mountaineer by bounding in great arcs down the vertical wall. Heather, clad only in a bikini top and the briefest of bicycle shorts, watched amazed as her dashing guide's loose-fitting T-shirt was suddenly sucked into his rappel device till the garment was stretched about his torso tight as the cellophane on a CD, nearly strangling him.

"Good gracious!" Nellie grumbled, quickly turning a couple wraps of the line round his leg. Now what . . . ? Just left, Nellie spotted a natty, frayed and corroded old #1 copperhead fixed in a grainy seam. He frantically threaded a sling through his harness, clipped off the old 'head, and eased his weight onto it and off his jammed ATC. Hysterical, Nellie drew a Swiss Army knife from his pocket, thumbed out the blade and, as his head started swimming from the shirt crimping his jugular, the Yosemite hardman took aim on the T-shirt and slashed away. His aim was excellent, and the next thing Nellie knew he'd shock-loaded onto the frayed #1 copperhead and the rope had twanged ten feet up and out of reach. He'd cut through his shirt, alright. He'd also cut clean through both strands of the rope.

The pair were perfectly stranded. Hysterical yells for help were heard, but because the sun had almost set, a rescue could not be mounted till the next morning so the dynamic duo spent the night just where they were: the beach-clad Heather trembling at the sling belay, and Nellie, his eyes like two exploding stars, studying the piano-wire copperhead—the only thing on God's earth keeping him from a horrible death, a

> ness may obtain of thee the God of all mercy perfect remission and forgiveness; through Jesus Christ our Lord. Amen. Almighty and everlasting God, who hatest nothing thou hast made, and dost forgive the sins of all those who are penitent; Create and make us in new and contrite hearts, that we, worthily lamenting our sins and acknowledging our wretchedness, may obtain of thee the God of all mercy, perfect remission and forgiveness; through Jesus Christ our Lord. Amen. Almighty and everlasting God, who hatest nothing thou hast made, and dost forgive the sins of all those who are penitent; Create and make us in new and contrite hearts, that

death he claims to have suffered roughly 10,000 times that long night.

COMMENTARY: Who can imagine spending the night some 400 feet up El Capitan suspended only by the manky and ever-so-thin cable of an old, #1 copperhead, a placement Nellie swore he saw (or imagined he saw) shift and rip from the seam over and over again throughout the livelong night.

PREVENTION: Take only experienced climbers onto world-class, multi-pitch climbs. Before rappelling, tuck in tight all shirts and anything else that can possibly be drawn into a rappel device. Using a knife anywhere near a weighted rope is always risky (when weighted a nylon rope cuts like string). If you must do it, use extreme caution.

# 19
# PRUSIK GRABS LIKE GRIM DEATH

*Bess left dangling in thin air*

Porgy and Bess had completed a basic climbing course under the aegis of the Sierra Club Rock Climbing Section and soon thereafter trudged up to Suicide Rock, near Idyllwild, California, with the intention of honing their rappelling skills. Once there, Porgy rigged a doubled rope off the three-bolt anchor on top of *Insomnia Crack*. However, the prospect of descending the free-hanging line shivered Porgy's timbers, so he extended Bess the courtesy of going first. Bess, a beautician and ex-mud wrestler who sported tattoos about her shoulders, brisket, one ass cheek, both ankles and several less conspicuous quarters, gingerly eased off the lip and began the 80-foot, airball rappel to the ground. Aside from a standard waist harness (rigged with a figure-8 descender), Porgy had set Bess up with a crude chest harness fashioned from two one-inch slings; to this he rigged a prusik knot attached to one strand of the rappel rope.

Thirty feet down the free-hanging rappel, part of Bess's loose-fitting T-shirt got sucked into the figure-8 descender. In an effort to pull the fabric free from the figure-8, Bess allowed her weight to shift entirely onto the aboriginal chest harness, which immediately slid up and locked tight around her arms and generous bosom. Unable to move her arms down to untangle the figure 8, and literally being squeezed to death by the constricting chest harness, Bess lost all feeling in her arms and within minutes was totally incapacitated. Paralyzed by the unforeseen problem, Porgy somehow managed to hail other climbers on the adjacent Sunshine Wall, and a rescue was quickly affected.

COMMENTARY: This mishap illustrates the dangers of a beginner using the prusik knot for "safety" reasons. The practice of using a jury-rigged chest harness with the prusik attached to one strand of the rappel rope is an oddball system I have never seen. Safety dictates that, should a climber choose to use a prusik knot as a backup for a rappel on a doubled rope, the prusik should be looped around both strands of the rope so they are weighted equally in the event that the rappeller loses control. Looping the prusik around only one strand is potentially fatal. Also, attach the prusik to the waist harness, not a chest harness.

PREVENTION: Tuck in all shirt tails before rappelling and never wear clothes that are baggy enough to get sucked into a rappel device. If Bess felt insecure about rappelling, she should have rappelled on a single rope doubled through the anchor (one rope, doubled, is long enough to accommodate this rappel) and had her partner belay her on the other rope. The last thing beginners want to do is needlessly complicate the system with questionable rigging (i.e. chest harness and prusik), especially rigging that they have no idea how to handle if a mishap occurs.

# 2.0

# FOR NUTS ONLY

*"Raked with a bastard file"*

Tobin and Ricky were attempting the first nuts-only ("clean") ascent of the South Face of Mount Watkins in Yosemite. Ricky, veteran of many Yosemite summers, was a masterful, discriminating cragsman. Tobin, though preternaturally skilled, was a quintessential maniac, a young man so reckless that his friends wondered how he had managed to live out his twenty-three years.

Per the route: the second pitch features a series of long pendulums that gain a pronounced left-facing dihedral. Ricky led up the pitch, reached the first bolt/pendulum point, lowered perhaps thirty feet, swung right to a second bolt, lowered and again swung right and into the corner; then he ascended the corner to a fixed belay.

Tobin began to follow the pitch on jumars. Upon reaching the first pendulum point, he should have rigged a backrope and casually rappelled down to the lower pendulum point; instead, the rash and incomprehensibly crazy Tobin simply unclipped from the bolt and jumped off. He plunged through the air in a dazzling, fifty-foot arc.

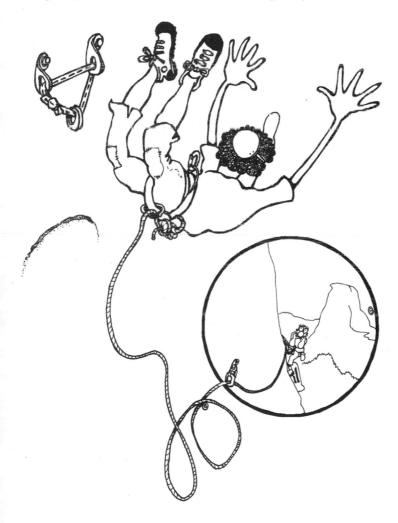

Astonishingly, his impulse flight resulted in only minor abrasions. With such success already under his swami belt, Tobin chose to repeat the jump when he reached the second pendulum point. However, this time he twirled, flopped, and bashed his way uncontrollably across the 80-degree wall, receiving flesh wounds that Ricky later described as "sickening to behold, as though his limbs had been raked with a bastard file."

COMMENTARY: A perfect example of bad judgment, and the willingness of a rash climber to needlessly endanger his life. The fact that Tobin became (arguably) the best overall climber of the 70s (flashing everything from the hardest free climbs to the grimmest big walls to vicious European alpine routes to Himalayan epics) does not diminish the inexplicable recklessness of this act.

PREVENTION: The standard procedure when cleaning long traverses is to rig a backrope off the pendulum point. This allows the second (the climber cleaning the pitch) to lower off, rather than simply unclip and jump—a jackass maneuver if ever there was one. The two normal backrope setups are: run the backrope through the pendulum point—that is, one end is tied off to your harness, feeds through the anchor, and runs back to you. By feeding rope out, you lower yourself over and down to the plumb line, where you can untie from the backrope and pull it through the anchor. Hazards include lowering directly off slings, which can burn through (it's always better to sacrifice a biner and run the rope through it), and somehow losing control of the end that is being fed through the pendulum point. If the wall is near or beyond vertical, much more force will be placed on the lower-off point than if you were on a lower-angled wall. Here it is often safer to double the backrope through the pendulum point and rappel down the plumbline, then pull the doubled rope through. In such instances it is safe to run the rope directly through a sling, since a rappel does not cause the weighted rope to grate over the nylon, as it does when lowering off. And remember to bear in mind that all fixed slings are suspect.

# 21

# INSUFFICIENTLY HUSKY

*Jammed line on the Whiteout*

Bart and Art were attempting an early free ascent of *Cotamundi Whiteout* on Granite Mountain, near Prescott, Arizona. They had completed the preliminary crack and corner pitches and, now at the 400-foot level, established a belay beneath the trademark roof that cuts across the top of the pallid granite crag. Bart led off the belay, hand-traversing left along a thin crack beneath the roof (5.11), his eyes darting between buttery smears, furtive pinches and the paltry, tied-off baby angle ostensibly protecting the moves. After about fifty feet, he set several large Friends, then jammed out and over the roof crack to a steep corner above. Suddenly, perhaps ten feet above the crux, the rope

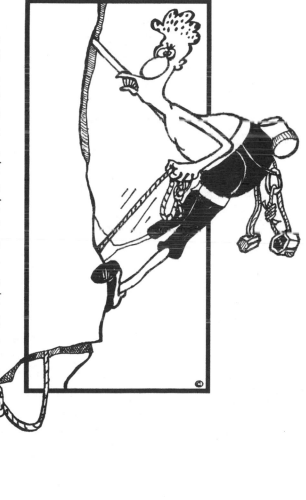

snagged in the roof. No amount of yanking could free it. Bart was able to secure himself to several wobbly hexcentrics, but judged this anchor "insufficiently husky" to belay Art over the laborious roof (solid 5.11), fearing Art might ping and pull them both off, plummeting to Jordan's Bank. Because the pair was climbing during a weekday, they were alone on the cliff and could not call for help. Art was left to make a series of half-rappels on the trail rope, and he'd nearly run out of gear by the time he gained the ground. Bart, in the meantime, remained anchored to the wall, 420 feet off the deck. It took Art an hour to hike around the back of the cliff to the top, secure an anchor and toss a line down to Bart; it took them the entire next day to reclimb the route, retrieve the gear left on the rappels and free the stuck rope from the roof.

COMMENTARY: This scenario illustrates the hazards of climbing a wandering route, where the rope follows exaggerated angles. Whenever a long traverse is followed by vertical climbing, there is always the chance of drastic rope drag at the juncture where the run of the rope changes from sideways to vertical. In the case of Bart and Art, this tendency was made worse by the ten-foot roof crack; not only did the rope make a 90-degree bend at the roof, but it also ran over an abrupt lip.

PREVENTION: Both the juncture where the route went from sideways to vertical, and the sudden bend at the lip of the roof crack, are places that a rope can jam and stop a climber cold if the protection has not been extended with slings. The problem is that nobody wants to clip long runners on pro plugged into a roof crack, because the length of the sling increases the length of any fall, and strenuous roofs tend to be adequately intimidating without the possibility of a longer-than-necessary fall. This route follows a rare but not unheard of geological line, and climbers do have to surmount such obstacles on occasion. Although *Cotamundi Whiteout* had been bagged many times with a single lead rope, using slings at all the sharp angles, it had become common practice over time for the leader to use twin lines, one for protecting the traverse, and the other for the roof. This is often a good option. In any event, on anything but short sport routes, a stuck line can involve wearisome and dangerous shenanigans for the climbing team to extricate themselves. When other climbers are present it is almost always safer to seek assistance, rather than to have to execute a series of short rappels off less-than-bomber protection, as Art did.

# 22

# SWISS GRIPPED ON THE DOME

*"Sheest! Dees line is bullsheet!"*

Two Swiss climbers, Franz and Feldspar, were completing a one-day ascent of the *Regular Route (Northwest Face)* on Half Dome. Franz had just led the exciting Thank God Ledge pitch; Feldspar followed, free climbing. Once Feldspar had traversed most of the way across the ledge, he noticed a loop of slack in the rope and yelled to Franz to "take" (take up rope).

Franz pulled on the lead rope, but it jammed behind a flake. Because it was late in the day and the pair were close to the top, Franz (a former national-level hammerthrower for the Swiss team) chose not to rappel down and free the jammed line; rather, he pulled harder still and managed to jam the cord so tight that Feldspar, pulling from his own end, was unable to free it.

What to do? With no choice but to abandon the stuck rope, Feldspar set up an anchor on his stance, and Franz set out to lead the next pitch, belayed only on an 8 mm trail line that the party had been using to haul a small pack containing water, various nougats, pâté, and the panoply of other funky provisions that Europeans mistake for grub. According to Franz, said haul line was in sad repair, having been used throughout the previous winter to secure kindling in the back of Feldspar's pickup. And it was on this very sad line that the Swiss mountaineers completed their ascent of Half Dome in what Feldspar described as the most frightening climbing of his career.

COMMENTARY: Almost without exception, when a line is stuck, excessive yanking will only ensure that the rope will never be freed.

PREVENTION: There is no way that the leader or belayer can keep an eye on the rope at all times. Sometimes the rope is completely out of sight, and it gets stuck—this happens to everybody eventually. However, when the line got stuck on the Swiss mountaineers, the only sane thing to do would have been for Franz to tie Feldspar off, then rappel down and attempt to free the snag by whatever means possible. Violent yanking is not a first resort but a last resort, to be tried only when all other methods have proved fruitless.

# 23

# DIVING OFF THE CAPTAIN

*Saved by the hand of God*

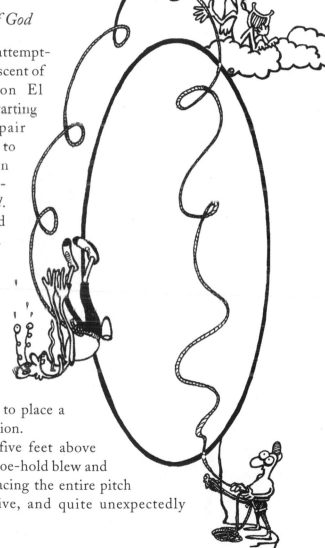

Mike and John were attempting the first one-day ascent of the *Triple Direct* on El Capitan, Yosemite. Starting before dawn, the pair jumared fixed ropes to Mammoth Ledges, ten pitches up the spectacular *Salathé Wall*. Here they roped up and John (world-renowned for recklessness) cast off at speed, dashing over 5.7 face climbing. After fifty feet, the terrain steepened and the difficulty increased to 5.9. John didn't break stride.

Nor did he pause to place a single piece of protection.

Perhaps seventy-five feet above Mammoth Ledges, a toe-hold blew and John pitched off, retracing the entire pitch in a perfect swan dive, and quite unexpectedly wrenching to a stop mere feet above Mike's head. Miraculously he was unhurt; however, his mind had melted into a quivering gray puddle, and he downclimbed a few feet to the belay.

Mike was confounded: What had arrested John's fall? The rope appeared to be snagged about thirty-five feet above. Mike flipped the rope once, and it snaked down to the ledges. There was no visible horn, flake, or crack that the rope could have snagged on—nothing. Mike swears he suddenly heard the sound of harps and fifes lofting on the breeze. The team immediately rappelled to the ground.

COMMENTARY: The notion of needlessly running the rope out on a big wall is a poor one. On long routes, half-a-day's climbing usually puts a team 500 or 600 feet off the deck, and out of immediate access to rescue.

PREVENTION: Over the first fifty feet of climbing, John had passed up many opportunities to slot protection, but couldn't be bothered because he is a 5.12 climber. He is also a very lucky man not to have killed himself when the toe-hold broke and he came flying off. Perhaps the fall was unavoidable, but had John set adequate pro, the monstrous whistler might instead have been a harmless, ten-foot skidder, and the pair could have carried on and made the first one-day ascent of one of America's most traveled walls. Instead the team was so rattled they had to retreat.

# 24

# HIKERS FILCH THORNTON'S LINE

*Sun nearly sets on Sunshine Wall*

A wave of roped soloing had swept through Suicide Rock in southern California, the edging capital of the USA, and the rush was on to see who could solo the bleakest routes. The method adopted by all soloists was: secure one end of the lead rope to an anchor, pull up several ten-to-fifteen foot loops of rope, and attach these to the harness by way of knots and biners. As the soloist scaled upward and a good foothold or ledge was gained, loops were dropped and added as needed. This was a crude but somewhat effective system, though on particularly grim routes, obliging footholds were scarce and fiddling with the loops often proved dicier than the climbing moves themselves. And because some of the more infamous routes featured runouts upwards of a nautical mile, the soloist was called upon repeatedly to "tighten up his sack" and carry on.

In any event, 5.11 routes were starting to fall to the roped soloers, particularly our man Thornton, whose pacific demeanor and simian strength were invaluable to the work. Zealous to add another "first" to his ledger, Thornton drove up to Suicide on a Wednesday and started up *New Generations*, a grave 5.11+ crimper route that takes a courageous line up the Sunshine Face, a 300-foot, high-angle slab of drooping knobs and scarce edges. In several hours, *New Generations* was a done thing.

Upon reaching the summit, Thornton tied his rope off to a tree and rappelled down to his last belay, which was at the start of the route's third and final pitch; this was standard practice, the purpose of which was to free the rope he had tied off to the three-bolt hanging belay anchor, and to clean the gear he'd placed while leading the pitch. At the belay, Thornton secured himself by way of slings and untied the end of the rope from the biners. Following procedure, he planned to tie into the end of the rope and reclimb the pitch, removing the pro and, whenever he saw fit, giving himself a belay by tying himself into the toprope via knots connected to biners on his harness.

But just as he was fixing to tie the end back into his harness, the very cord was yanked from his mitts. Woefully, he watched as the end snaked its way up the wall

CLOSE CALLS

and threatened to disappear over the lip. Thornton cursed ardently; the rope stopped moving. Words were subsequently exchanged between Thornton—anxiously runnered-off to three bolts, 250 feet up a naked wall of rock—and several hikers who had scrambled up a gully to the top of the wall, where Thornton's line was secured to the block. The hikers had apparently seen the line, assumed it abandoned and proceeded to reel in their booty. Thornton nervously explained to the hikers—who were out of sight and some ways back from the frightful lip—that lest they drop the rope back down to him, they would leave him stranded.

The embarrassed hikers obliged, but for their finest efforts they couldn't flip, jiggle, cajole or pitch the rope down to the exact location of Thornton's belay. Several times the rope snaked down just beyond Thornton's grasp, and several times he considered unclipping from the anchor and soloing over to the line; but for the burnished warts and glossy nothings afforded by the flanking stone, and the image of a toe blowing off and Thornton plunging to his Maker, he could not bring himself to unclip from the anchor and solo across the wall to fetch the cord.

Thornton was left high and dry. On such a weekday as this, the crag was nigh vacant, and several tense hours passed before the hikers were able to locate another climber, who in turn rapped down to Thorton and offered him the end of his rope.

COMMENTARY: This episode is proof that the most improbable things can happen. One would think that hikers would realize someone had reason to leave an expensive-looking rope dangling down a cliff known for technical climbing—but we can never underestimate the stupidity, greed, or innocence of our brethren.

PREVENTION: In normal lead-climbing situations, there is always someone tied to both ends of the line, so the chance of strangers filching said line from the climbing team is zero.

However, when any rope is left secured to an anchor on top of a cliff, it presents an open invitation for any passersby to start fiddling about with the rigging or even pinch the unattended line. While in Thornton's case it was probably impractical to post a note saying that the rope was in use, and that his life depended on it remaining just as it was, a note was probably the only thing that would have prevented the hikers from reeling in his life line.

# 25

# RODENTS RIP RUBY'S ROPE

*Gnawed to the quick on the Big Stone*

Yolanda and Ruby spent five grueling days hammering up the cruel ramparts of the *Aquarian Wall*, El Capitan, Yosemite. On the afternoon of the sixth day, the duo gained Thanksgiving Ledge, which cuts across the left side of the wall several hundred feet below the summit. Thrashed from the preceding climbing, and finding their gear—and their nerves—fairly shot, they chose to quit for the day, reorganize their gear, devour the last of their fodder and kick it on the roomy ledge to enjoy the sunset. With only a short 5.10a crack and some fourth-class friction separating them from the summit, they figured to pass a luxurious night log-sawing on the ledge and to top out early the next day.

Both climbers slept like Pharaohs, and the following morning both were anxious to summit and return to the cush living for which the Valley is renown. However, as

Ruby flaked out the cord to belay Yolanda on this last pitch to grandeur, Ruby discovered that rodents (most likely rats) had nibbled the line so tragically that in over a dozen spots the core was gnawed half through. They frantically checked the haul line and discovered the same thing—it too was gnawed down to a kite string in a dozen spots. They spread both ropes out on the ledge and found that neither line was sound for more than twenty feet. Though both Yolanda and Ruby were apprentice wall climbers, both were free-climbing machines, and both had made free ascents of the daring *West Face* route, which summited several hundred feet left along the ledge. Ruby considered: their ropes were probably good enough to haul the bags with, but neither climber was keen to lead on them, nor were they eager to lead straight off via a series of twenty-foot pitches. So the pair lugged the haulbag left along Thanksgiving Ledge to the exit chimneys on the *West Face* route. Here, Ruby tied both ropes together and soloed easy 5.7 ground to the rounded summit, where she hauled the bag as Yolanda soloed beneath it, pushing it along when it jammed in the tapering bowels of the chimney.

COMMENTARY: The ways that a rope can get damaged on a long climb are many, but damage by varmints is one of the least likely.

PREVENTION: Astute rope management is crucial on long climbs. Big walls require at the minimum both a lead and a haul rope, and the probability of both lines getting damaged is relative to many factors. The nature of the rock (coarse, smooth, etc.) and the zigs and zags the route takes (which contribute to abrasion possibilities) are primary hazards. Keeping a rope in good shape is largely a case of predicting and avoiding the situations where the line can get worked. Staying "on the ball" is key—for instance, when you see the line is snaking over a sharp edge, you extend the pro with a runner or take other precautionary measures. But predicting the unpredictable (such as hungry rats or a meteor strike) is the job of a seer, not a mountaineer. To safeguard against the unpredictable, many wall climbers always lap-coil the rope while belaying and coil all loose rope during every bivouac. In the case of rodents, the only insurance is to stuff the lines in tooth-proof bags which contain no food residue. Most experienced wall climbers intuitively ask themselves, per every situation, the following question: What could possibly go wrong here? They then take every measure to keep things safe and secure.

# 26

# DOG DAYS AT SMITH ROCKS

*"Horny" had a hunger*

The only thing longer than Loomis and Mort's partnership was Loomis's relationship with his dog, Horny, a mongrel of ambiguous parentage who loved to ravage perfumed lap dogs, and who rode in the back of Loomis's Toyota pickup when Loomis and Mort were crag bound. Following a grueling day at Smith Rocks, Loomis and Mort tossed their packs in the back of Loomis's pickup

and motored toward Bend. As usual, Horny stood sentinel in the back. When the duo reached home, Mort no sooner snatched his rucksack and shouldered it than various strands of his lead rope—gnawed clean through—spilled out a formidable hole in the bottom of his pack.

**COMMENTARY:** Loomis and Mort had spent the entire day frigging up a sport climb. Horny was left to watch this demonstration with a bowl of water but no food. Riding home, the ravenous cur caught wind of a half-finished sandwich in the bottom of Mort's pack and went to work, teeth first.

**PREVENTION:** A "climbing" accident? Not hardly. But one thing's for sure: whenever storing food and gear in the same pack, make certain the grub cannot mingle with gear. Use ziplocked bags inside another stuff sack. I've had tuna oil saturate ropes and foul biners. Any loose food will attract ants, squirrels or starving mutts.

# 27

# GRANITE PINBALL

*Bombs away on the East Buttress*

Horatio and I were climbing the *East Buttress* of Middle Cathedral, an exciting trade route up the steep and creamy flanks of this wondrous monolith. Because it was a busy summer weekend we'd planned to start early, hoping to get a jump on the four or five teams that are usually found on the route on any given day. However, Horatio was nursing a cruel hangover brought on by consuming vast quantities of "Jungle Juice," an explosive and debilitating concoction consisting of fruit punch and Everclear. Consequently, we didn't rope up till 8 A.M., and a European team was starting the third pitch by the time we gained the first belay.

Though this classic line has seen hundreds of ascents over the years, loose rock remains on either side of the climbing route, a fact spelled out by the annual accident reports describing rocks pelting and even seriously injuring folks on the *East Buttress*. We were directly below and in the line of fire of the Europeans; however, we gambled and carried on, Horatio laboring under a "head" big as an apartment complex. An hour passed. Just after dusting off the bolt ladder on the third pitch, I heard yelling from above, where the Euros were groping up the crumbly flare on the fifth lead.

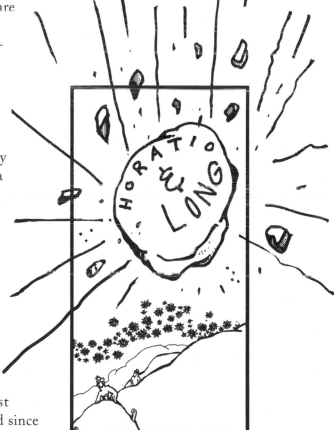

Then came the percussive rattling of a big stone bounding our way.

With no place to take cover, I stuffed my nose into a wee corner as Horatio froze on the belay ledge directly below. In a flash, a large rock exploded on the ledge several feet left of Horatio, flying shards ripping into his legs. After screaming terrified promises of torture and death to whoever kicked off so much as another pea, Horatio discovered that our rope had been chopped half through. Since the gash was almost dead-center in the line, and since we didn't have a spare, I gingerly frigged down the bolt ladder back to the belay ledge. We couldn't lead on the chopped line, nor could we rap off. In an hour, a trio of Persian climbers reached us, and we climbed off with them.

COMMENTARY: As illustrated several times in this book, it is always a gamble to climb beneath another party. Even on glacier-polished slab routes featuring nothing at all to pull off, climbers still drop biners and other gear that quickly gain enough velocity to strike your person with the might of a .44 slug. Horatio and I had both climbed the *East Buttress* many times before, and we both knew the route had loose rock from top to bottom. We knew it was even money that the team climbing above us would yank off something and that we'd be directly in the line of fire. We gambled and lost—fortunately, we lost only a rope and not our lives. A few feet either way and I wouldn't be sitting here hacking out these words.

PREVENTION: The only certain way to avoid getting bombed by rocks from a party climbing above is to stay off the climb. The problem is that on trade routes like the *East Buttress* of Middle Cathedral, folks queue up halfway to Modesto, waiting to get cracking. So lest you bivy at the base and start up at first light, a team is likely to already be climbing by the time even the earliest bird reaches the base. On popular, multiday big walls, even this go-first-or-not-at-all strategy won't work because there are often teams on the wall that started the previous day, and if you waited for them to top out, ten other teams would have launched their ascent in the meantime. During peak months (especially on weekends), climbers usually have to share the trade routes with others. If you take this gamble, verbally make your presence known to any parties above and, if possible, request that they warn you before launching onto loose terrain. This, of course, is not always possible (say, when a team is ten pitches above you). Again, climbing below other parties is always a gamble.

CLOSE CALLS

On sound rock the gamble is often worth taking, providing the upper team doesn't drop a Gri-Gri on your bean; but to follow another team up a junk pile is to "let the Devil into your bedroom."

# 28

# NO KNOT ON THE NOSE

*Rock stars make do with nothing*

Richard Harrison and Nick Escort were at the chilling hanging belay one lead above Camp Six, the *Nose*, Yosemite. A Stonemaster, Richard had many big walls under his harness; a renowned English mountaineer, Nick had championed numerous Himalayan summits. They reckoned there was no manner of terrain between Yosemite Valley and the Hindu Kush that one or the other of them could not dick. Such was their thinking when they teamed up for the *Nose*—thinking confirmed by their fluid progress up the noblest stone on earth.

And so it was in the rarefied air of the Captain's upper dihedrals that Richard handed Nick the sling of gear to begin leading the next pitch. Nick smiled a toothy grin as he clasped the knotted nylon runner and prepared to cast off. His smile froze as the knot in the sling came loose and the bulk of the teams leading gear slid free. Dumbfounded, Nick and Richard watched helplessly as the rack upon which their lives depended dropped 2,600 feet down the wall and rattled into the talus below.

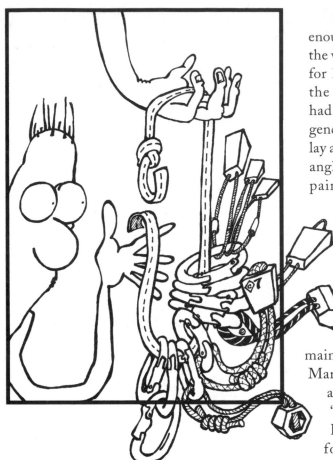

Scrambling to put together enough gear to get their asses off the wall, they dug in the haulbag for loose nuts. Nick broke out the half-dozen pegs Richard had brought along for an emergency, and they trimmed the belay anchor down to one standard angle. Through this process the pair concocted a paltry rack consisting of several small wired nuts, four large hexes, and the six pegs—four of which were blades and horizontals. With said rack, it took the duo two long days to accomplish the remaining 500 feet to the summit. Many times they ran out of gear after climbing a very brief "pitch." In a typical scenario, Richard would aid up a uniform 1-inch crack, leap frogging a #7 Stopper and a 1-inch angle (with a broken eye) while hearing the clashing of pitchforks echoing in his head. After forty feet, with nothing between him and the anchor—which, excepting fixed anchors, usually consisted of nothing more than a #3 wired Stopper or a rusty piton—Richard simply ran out of hair and rigged another improbable hanging belay off another wired nut, an experience he later claimed would "fill the trousers of a bronze statue."

They were able to "clean" several fixed pins and nuts along the way, which bolstered their rack somewhat, but they reached the summit bolt-ladder none too soon. From the pitch above Camp Six (where the gear was lost) to the summit is a span usually done in six pitches; it took Richard and Nick nearly twenty abbreviated (not to mention exceedingly dangerous) leads to accomplish the same.

COMMENTARY: Dropping ropes and various bits of gear is certainly not unheard of, even for experienced climbers; dropping the odd nut or pin is something that happens to every climber at sometime in their career. (A famous English climber once dropped his boots off the fourth pitch of El Cap's *North American Wall* route.) Stuff comes unclipped, is kicked off ledges, or slips through battered hands. One can only hope that whatever's dropped will not make or break the ascent—or set one up for a harrowing epic like Richard and Nick endured.

PREVENTION: Dropping gear is not only a costly mistake, it's a liability to anyone below. And on long routes, it's a liability to the climbing team relative to how much and how crucial the gear was that got dropped. Many wall climbers clip racks off with locking biners to minimize the freaky chance of the rack coming unclipped and plunging away. Keeping everything clipped in at all times is absolutely essential—and it's also impossible, because if you never unclipped anything, you'd never be able to move. So obviously the biggest danger lies in the transition time when one unclips something from one point and clips it into another. That's why this transition requires extreme vigilance.

When handing the rack off to a partner, most experienced wall climbers look the other climber in the eye and won't unclasp the rack till their partner is looking them in the eye and says, "I've got it." Some won't unclasp it till it's actually around the partner's shoulder or clipped onto their rack. In the case of Nick and Richard, even this strategy wouldn't have helped since the sling itself came untied—one of the reasons that tied slings are mostly a thing of the past. Ultimately, the safest system keeps everything clipped off whenever possible, with clusters of gear (racks, etc.) secured via locking biners. Anything loose is not long for the vertical world. Never set anything down unsecured on a bivy or belay ledge, as you or your partner will invariably knock it off. And whenever handling gear freely in your hands—especially when handing the gear to a partner—always be aware that this is the time when gear is most often dropped.

# 29

# GERTY SKIDS THE PLANK

*Blazing buns on Captain Hook*

Gertrude and Amos were attempting the one-pitch route *Captain Hook* on the north side of Suicide Rock, southern California. The route, a longtime favorite among intermediate climbers, follows a vertical flake gaping from the wall, inside of which the climber battles upward via unctuous chimneying. Following tradition, leader Gertrude liebacked up the first ten feet and pulled into the bombay chimney—without stopping to slot protection. As the climbing beyond was rated only 5.7, and because the crack—far back in the depths of the flare—begrudgingly accepts small wired nuts, Gertrude hastily placed a small brass microwedge and carried on.

Several feet above, Gertrude somehow lost her counterpressure and skidded downward, much as a person rides a toboggan down a sheer snow slope—except here the snow was granite flecked with warts and rugosities, and Gertrude's taut but supple caboose served as the

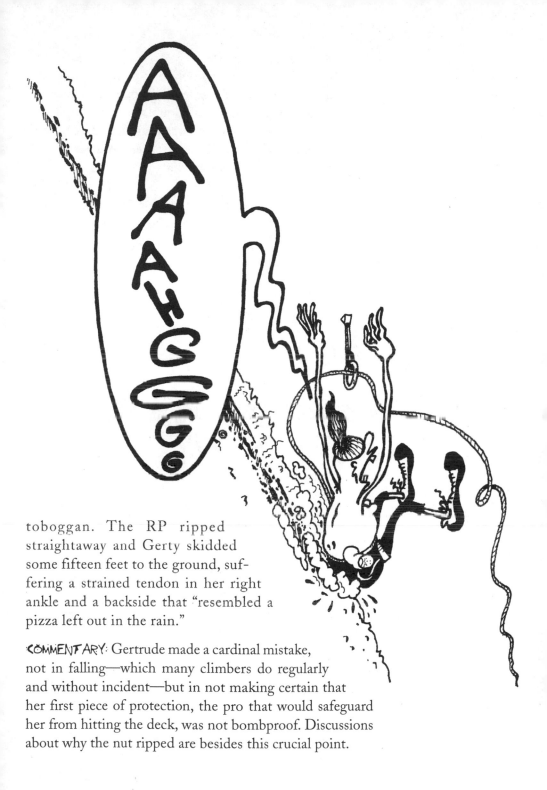

toboggan. The RP ripped straightaway and Gerty skidded some fifteen feet to the ground, suffering a strained tendon in her right ankle and a backside that "resembled a pizza left out in the rain."

COMMENTARY: Gertrude made a cardinal mistake, not in falling—which many climbers do regularly and without incident—but in not making certain that her first piece of protection, the pro that would safeguard her from hitting the deck, was not bombproof. Discussions about why the nut ripped are besides this crucial point.

PREVENTION: When there is only one piece of protection separating a leader from a groundfall, that piece must be placed with radical caution, and doubled or even tripled up if there seems to be the slightest chance it might fail if fallen on—and sometimes even if it doesn't seem so. The fact that the climbing above is easier than that just cranked is no guarantee that you will not fall off. Some climbers routinely place a minimum of two pieces of pro at their first stance. It can't be emphasized enough that the first piece of pro slotted above the ground must be fail-safe or backed up—this is the only sure way to avoid the dreaded groundfall.

# 30

# FERDY'S FINGERS BUTTER OFF

*Tarred and feathered but still kicking*

Ferdy and Norbert were working out the fierce moves on *Tar and Feathers*, at Suicide Rock, a short (sixty-foot) but taxing (5.12a) lieback that follows a paper-thin, left-slanting flake. Though the initial moves (continuous 5.11) are grim duty, most leaders find the climbing easier than placing good or even tolerable pro in the expanding flake. Ferdy and Norbert had both taken several turns leading, and a high point had been reached perhaps thirty feet up. Ferdy went up for a third try, cranking to their highpoint (a #6 Stopper) and moving a body length higher. As he hung off his fingertips trying desperately to place a small TCU, his fingers buttered off and he pitched downward like a stuntman fired from a cannon, ripping all his pro out and slamming into the ground. Amazingly, Ferdy escaped with only a cracked rib and a bruised kidney.

COMMENTARY: The problem of protecting this climb is well established. Owing to the flared nature of the crack, bottleneck placements are scarce, as are parallel sections that would accept a stout camming device. The problem is magnified by the fact that the crack leans, and a falling climber puts oblique stress on the already marginal pro.

PREVENTION: What to do? First, understand that tackling routes such as *Tar and Feathers* is a calculated risk. At best, the protection is questionable simply due to the lack of ideal placements. Add to this the odd-angled forces placed on the gear in the event of a fall, and you have an accident waiting to happen.

One option is that after the leader reaches a highpoint and lowers down (gingerly) to the ground, the belayer can lock him off while the leader bounces on the rope and tests the pro from the relative safety of terra firma. At the very least this can verify if the top piece is sound enough to catch a short fall. If the top piece rips, take up rope to the next lower piece and weight that one, and so forth until one holds. When I made an early ascent of this route, I followed this procedure and proceeded to rip every nut from the crack when testing them. Obviously, extreme caution is required on routes of this kind. And when testing the pro from the ground, make sure that if the nut pops you don't tumble backward onto rugged terrain—a very real possibility.

# 31

# NABISCO FLYER

*Ozzie takes the swing*

Ozzie and Harriet were attempting *Wheat Thin*, the second pitch of the illustrious Nabisco Wall on the Cookie Cliff in Yosemite. The pair had already climbed the strenuous *Waverly Wafer* pitch (5.10c) and were secured to a bolted belay on a small, tapering ledge that extended some fifteen feet right to the start of the *Wheat Thin* pitch. This famous and photogenic pitch consists of a vertical lieback up an exfoliating flake.

As Harriet belayed, Ozzie moved directly right toward the start of the flake and slotted a small wired nut. Climbing directly up and past the nut, he began the tricky (5.10c) face moves that gain the flake proper. A young man of immense strength and little intelligence, Ozzie's feet were a meter above the nut when he bungled the crux

move and popped. The nut ripped out and Oz's huge pendulum fall described no less grand an arc than those performed by trapeze artists under the Big Top.

His brain rattled and his torso peppered with wicked abrasions, Ozzie finally came to a stop some twenty-five feet below Harriet.

COMMENTARY: When Oz began the tricky face moves toward the flake, the rope was running about fifteen feet directly right to the wire. As he started up, the rope was at a 90-degree angle from belayer to nut to the direction he was climbing. When he fell off, direct sideways force was placed on the nut, lifting it from an otherwise bombproof slot.

PREVENTION: Oz's mistake was that he went with a single wired nut, rather than rigging a directional, which would have absorbed the lateral forces (as it has for twenty years worth of climbers falling off exactly the same spot). Following any traverse, the first piece of protection must be a directional, usually accomplished by placing a nut for an upward pull and connecting it to the down-slotted nut. Without the directional, even the best nut is prone to pull out when shock-loaded with an oblique pull.

# 32

# HELLUVA TIME ON MT. DUTZI

*"Blockhead" Lucifer and the desert serpent*

Lucifer and Mo were attempting a new route on the South Face of Mount Dutzi, in Joshua Tree. Lucifer had climbed about fifty feet up moderate but unprotected rock to a thin crack, placed a camming device, and traversed ten feet up and right over difficult (5.11) rock to a small foothold stance. Several feet farther right was a second crack in which Lucifer hoped to secure much-needed protection. Owing to rope drag, Lucifer gave several stout tugs on the cord and, to his utter horror, watched the camming unit he'd placed rotate from the crack and slide down the rope.

So there he stood, balanced precariously on an edge so small it wouldn't hold a jelly bean, with nothing between himself and the naked deck sixty feet below. He was only several tantalizing feet away from the next crack, but because the climbing ahead looked even harder than the 5.11 moves he'd already cranked, the sniffling Lucifer categorically ruled out continuing on without pro. It was hastily decided that Mo would race around the dome, scramble up third-class slabs to the top (the dome is only 150 feet high) and drop Lucifer down a toprope. Since they only had one rope, Lucifer was forced to untie and balance ropeless on the stance, a position he could maintain only by continually shifting and changing feet. This terrifying two-step continued for what seemed like an eternity, but in reality it was only ten minutes before Mo gained the top of the dome and positioned himself directly above Lucifer.

The real fun, it turned out, had yet to begin. While Mo was anchoring the rope off to a large block, he disturbed a diamondback rattler, which promptly bit him on the calf. Mo panicked, and a desperate conversation ensued between Mo—doubled over with a rattlesnake bite— and Lucifer, ropeless and gripped, standing on a wee stance so very far above the hungry boulders.

Ten minutes later, after Lucifer had convinced the rapidly deteriorating Mo that they would both surely perish if he didn't drop him a line, Mo heroically accomplished the task and Lucifer handwalked up the rope. It took the pair nearly an hour to get off the dome and back to the car, and an additional hour before Mo was admitted to the emergency room at Twenty Nine Palms, some forty miles distant, where the serpent's toxins could be neutralized by a single shot of antivenin, a treatment which touched Mo to the tune of $236.

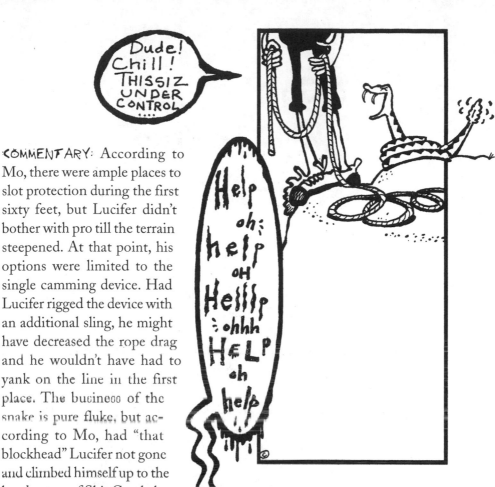

**COMMENTARY:** According to Mo, there were ample places to slot protection during the first sixty feet, but Lucifer didn't bother with pro till the terrain steepened. At that point, his options were limited to the single camming device. Had Lucifer rigged the device with an additional sling, he might have decreased the rope drag and he wouldn't have had to yank on the line in the first place. The business of the snake is pure fluke, but according to Mo, had "that blockhead" Lucifer not gone and climbed himself up to the headwaters of Shit Creek, he, Mo, would never have gotten bitten. Yet another case of an experienced climber taking a few things for granted and nearly paying for it with everything.

**PREVENTION:** Traversing puts oblique forces on vertically oriented protection. Many climbers double up such placements, and most climbers strive to make each piece of pro (when sideways moves are involved) multidirectional to compensate for the lateral shock-loading. And anyone who starts out on 5.11 face moves with only one piece protecting a sixty-foot groundfall is playing Russian roulette.

# 33

# LUCKY SKIPS THE CLIP

*Lucky logs a fall*

Lucky was a semi-honed sport climber who relished the chance to dangle on the roof of the local climbing gym. Though portly, Lucky had a bold streak that sometimes led to trouble; however, due to the gym's fixed pro (a bolt every four feet or so), Lucky had never gotten scratched despite his penchant for occasionally skipping clips. This latter practice caught up with him, however.

Feeling sharp after some warm-up laps on crimpy toprope problems, Lucky moved to the gigantic arch that is this gym's centerpiece. Routes following the inside of the arch start on 110-degree terrain and turn to dead horizontal after twenty feet. Lucky started up a series of rigorous crimps and reachy cross-overs. As is usual with grim gym routes, the first clip was positioned by a good hold, and Lucky managed it fine. At the second clip, however, Lucky found himself staring at the bolt with his arms crossed, reckoning his only chance at flashing the route was to bypass the bolt (rather than stop in an awkward position and try to clip the biner, a procedure that can sap strength). Lucky skipped the clip and carried on.

At the third clip (where the wall had kicked back to 130 degrees) Lucky found himself in the same position: staring at the bolt with his hands crossed. He could not skip this bolt as well, so, hanging off a doigit, he pulled up slack and promptly pinged off. Because he had skipped

the second clip and had pulled out additional length of rope to attempt to clip the third bolt, Lucky unluckily had far too much line out for the first bolt to arrest his fall.

Lucky augured into the mat and sprained both ankles.

COMMENTARY: With many gym climbs, it is usually the second bolt that safeguards a groundfall. Once a climber is established high on the route—with five or six bolts clipped beneath him/her—skipping a beastly clip is sometimes done to save strength for the actual moves. However, skipping lower clips, especially the first three, is dangerous—especially if the climbing is at or near your limit.

PREVENTION: One simple rule: never skip clips, indoors or out.

# 34

# DOPE ON THE TOPROPE

*"He carved through space like a trapeze geek"*

Rudy and Harry were taking turns pumping out laps on a wildly overhanging gym route that followed the contours of an inverted, horseshoe-shaped arch. After six laps apiece, they were too hosed to keep leading the route, known for it's strenuous clips, and instead opted to toprope

a few more laps. That is, the climber tied into the free end of the rope as the belayer belayed the end that snaked through the dozen or so draws. Owing to the overhanging nature of the climb, the top anchor was situated at least twenty feet horizontally from where the climb started—in other words, the route overhung about twenty feet, so when Rudy began his toprope attempt, he risked a huge, free-air pendulum if he pinged.

And sure enough, Rudy was barely ten feet up the route when his hands gave out and away he went, "carving through space like a trapeze geek" as he puts it. The gym was crowded, as gyms frequently are, and as Rudy swooped low across the rug he broadsided another climber who reported seeing stars and constellations for two days afterwards.

COMMENTARY: Following a route someone else has led in the gym is common practice (though prohibited in many gyms), especially for people not yet cleared to lead, for children and for those wanting to try routes too difficult (meaning too strenuous to accomplish the clips) to lead themselves. Toprope routes usually serve this purpose, but people tire of the same moves and naturally want to match—as best they can—the exploits of the big girls and boys. This and other reasons lead people to follow an indoor lead. On a straight, up-and-down line there is no worry. But when folks start trying to follow wildly overhanging jug hauls on the free end of the rope—meaning the strand of the doubled rope that is NOT clipped through the bolts—wild swings are in the offing if the follower peels off while still low on the route. Why would someone try to follow this way? Again, it allows them to attempt the moves without having to waste gas unclipping.

PREVENTION: To clarify the picture: Jacki leads a wildly overhanging gym route, reaches the anchor and lowers off. She unties, and her partner Trish ties in. The rope runs from Trish up to the belay anchor on top, then back down through the protection bolts to the other end—the end that Jacki now belays on. When Trish starts up, she's starting on holds that are, say, twenty horizontal feet away from the plum line of the belay anchor. If she comes off down low, she's going to swing "like a trapeze geek." If there's nothing but air to hit, there's no harm in taking this swing (commonly known as a "rug burner"). But in the case of Rudy, other bodies were in harm's way and a price was paid.

Whenever trying this practice, always make certain no one is around. Toproping severely overhanging gym climbs is dangerous when people are anywhere near the path of a potential pendulum fall. And just because nobody is in the line of fire when you start up doesn't mean someone won't wander into body-slamming range during the attempt. If there is *any* chance of swinging into someone, notify the crowd; or better yet, move to a designated toprope area, where the routes have been engineered to avoid such swings.

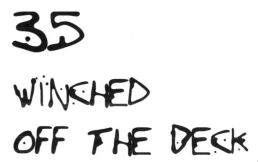

# 35

# WINCHED OFF THE DECK

*They smacked like clackers*

Thelma and Louise were attempting to climb an overhanging route following a line of widely spaced buckets. Louise led, instructing Thelma to get braced for a possible fall, since the route had thwarted Louise three times before, and because she had a stalwart frame, a yen for

Mongolian bar-b-que (of which she had recently indulged herself), and consequently, outweighed Thelma by some fifty pounds.

Thelma dug in her heels: Louise started up. After twenty feet, the route bent back to near horizontal. Louise hucked a long dyno, missed the hold and flew off. The force of the fall winched Thelma off the deck and payed perhaps five additional feet of rope into the system. As Louise swung back into the plumb line, Thelma rose to meet her and the pair smacked like clackers. The impact opened a gash above Thelma's eyebrow, compliments of Louise's elbow.

**COMMENTARY**: Both climbers were experienced and knew better than to have the belayer try to get by with no anchor. Caught in the moment, busy with trying to sustain a decent pump, the duo skipped a standard procedure and Thelma got twelve stitches to show for it.

**PREVENTION**: When the leader outweighs the belayer by more than fifteen pounds (rope friction will compensate for a slight weight disparity), the belayer should always anchor off and position herself in the line of pull. This is standard procedure inside the gym and out at the cliffs. Many consider a ground belay safe only when the belayer is anchored off—and there's no basis to dispute this philosophy, regardless of the relative weights of the climbers. An anchorless ground belay, if performed at all, should be limited to toproping situations, not leads.

# 36

# HANK FELT 'STRONG LIKE BULL'

*. . . Then the hold spun*

Hank worked a mile from the local climbing gym, and several times a week took his lunch breaks there, climbing routes if he could snag a partner, hand-traversing himself to smithereens if the place was empty. The accident happened on one of Hank's hand-traversing days. Owing to a three-day layoff, he felt "strong like bull," determined to milk his entire lunch break on the wall—without once touching down.

The gym was empty as a political promise, so Hank commenced pumping out laps on the long and punishing hand traverse. As concrete slowly seeped into his guns, Hank found it troublesome to cling to the smallish holds. Nevertheless, he gritted his teeth and pushed. After several more laps, Hank's arms were perfectly turgid; Hank quickly traversed into a corner and, finding the holds skimpy, stemmed up a few body lengths to a back-step, no-hands rest. He bridged out and let his dead arms drop to his sides; suddenly, the right foothold spun and Hank flew off, falling fifteen feet to the deck and cracking a wrist.

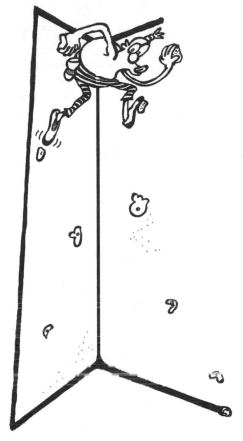

COMMENTARY: Hank experienced what every gym climber will eventually encounter: a hold that spins when weighted. Considering the traffic on most gym climbs, especially moderate routes, it's no surprise that certain holds (particularly those screwed onto sections of wall with surface irregularities) will work loose. Holds can be cranked only so tight without the risk of stripping the T-nut or cracking the hardened epoxy resin. Excepting competitions (where the course setters crank the holds down like crazy), gym operators are instructed not to overcrank the holds.

PREVENTION: Indoors and out, every bouldering fall is a "grounder," so never climb higher than where you can comfortably fall to the deck. This is especially important when cranking into awkward, crunchy positions, like back-step-ping or drop-kneeing. Falling out of such an unnatural position can result in a wide variety of leg and knee injuries. And when bouldering on overhanging turf, get a spot, because when you pop off you won't land on your feet, but your ass—and possibly your neck. Bad . . . .

In short, when bouldering indoors, beware of "spinners," particularly when traversing high off the deck or attempting to cop a no-hands rest.

# 37

# WHEN LANGSTON LOST IT

*Ankles away on the Gunnite Roof*

Langston was obsessed with a roof climb at his local gym, trying and flying off it repeatedly. Though the final twenty feet finished on handlebar holds, the initial sequence of rude doigits and slopers conspired to fry Langston before he could reach said jugs and Rambo through to the "summit." Once he'd come close, pitching off while trying to clip the anchors. Determined to bag the route before course setters removed it, Langston tied in once again and cast off, drifting over the difficult lower span with poise and gaining the generous holds with reasonable gas in reserve.

Rather than dash for the anchors, which had cost him before, Langston concentrated on shrewd footwork, heel-hooking now and again to unweight his ebbing guns. Near the lip he climbed past a ring bucket, hollow in the middle, and when the ring came within reach of his foot, he booted the whole of his shoe into the breech and promptly buttered off. His foot remained slotted in the ring bucket like a key in a lock and only torqued painfully out when Langston's head tilted straight down. Amazingly, Langston broke no bones, but his ankle required ligament surgery that kept him out of the gym for three months.

COMMENTARY: Most gyms feature at least a few holds that resemble nothing in the geological world—holds in the form of skulls, buffalo, starfish, a figure unknown to mankind, horseshoes, Model As, kitchen sinks and space shuttles. There are also various "ring" holds that resemble gymnastic rings. It is inviting, when massively pumped, to slot a foot THROUGH these rings, much as Langston did in the previous scenario.

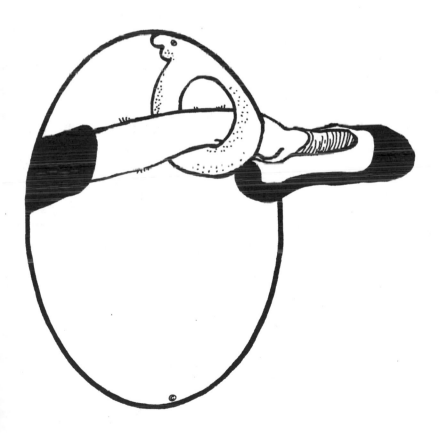

PREVENTION: Hooking these types of ring holds should only be done in a way that will allow your foot or arm to gently slide out should you fall. I've seen pumped climbers jam entire arms and legs through these rings and cringed at the thought of bodies flying off, leaving limbs behind. Whether inside or outside, keying a foot into a position where there is little or no play is a compound fracture waiting to happen. Instead, try to guide the foot in only so far that it will still be able to slide out in the event of a fall. Of course, a desperately pumped climber will often do just about anything to stay glued to the wall or cliff, but common sense must prevail; no climb is worth the gruesome potential outcome of slotting a limb thus. As a general rule, ring holds in the gym are safe only for fingers and toes. Anything more might get lodged and broken in a fall.

# 38

# THROBBING PATE

*Dead head from the deadpoint*

Marcus was the heir to a timber fortune and one of the smarmiest cads to ever don *klutterschues*. When Marcus wasn't betting on the ponies or prowling about various nudie bars around the Los Angeles International Airport, Marcus was pestering women and cranking 5.12 eliminators at the local rock gym. Marcus was a skilled if sometimes hysterical leader.

Marcus dropped by the rock gym one afternoon and shagged a belay from the gym owner's wife. Marcus launched up a bulging wall on a series of measly but satisfactory red gargoyles. Marcus matched hands on a sloper and glanced up, noticing that the next move required a long deadpoint. Marcus glanced down at his belayer and said, "Watch me—if you want to learn something." Marcus winked. Marcus hucked a long deadpoint. BONK! Marcus's head smacked into a green bollard hold, knocking him silly—though Marcus was impeccably silly to begin with. Marcus now had a three-stitch gash on his pate.

COMMENTARY: One of the curses of a gym that features ambitious course setters is that they often try to milk every inch of available wall space. The result—especially in toprope zones—is a lane of wall barely eight feet wide hosting perhaps six different routes. Picture the wall, spangled with blue, black, red, white, yellow and green holds, all of it as densely packed as the sprinkles on a cupcake—and all of it potentially "in the way" of the climber (and the climber's head). Though Marcus's mishap was something of a fluke, no active gym climber hasn't smacked a hand or rasped some hide on, say, a big green hold while slapping for a red hold. It smarts.

PREVENTION: Watch your head.

CLOSE CALLS

# 39

# FRANK'S FACE FRACTURED IN FLYING FIASCO

*They met by chance in midair*

Frank and Hank were both working up opposite sides of a horseshoe arch, the principal feature of this indoor gym. Once on the underside of the arch, both climbers proceeded over burly, horizontal gunnite, climbing toward each other. While the respective routes did not cross, they passed close, perhaps six feet apart, going opposite directions. Yarding upside down, Frank and Hank yarded past each other at midarch and wobbled on, working out the moves on trifling holds, struggling with the clips.

Presently, when the climbers were about twenty feet apart, Frank pitched off, followed almost immediately by Hank. When they wrenched onto the bolts, their pendulum falls sent them swinging through midair and back toward each other. They collided, and Frank's face smacked into Hank's knee. The impact cracked the orbital bone below Frank's eye (the classic "boxer's" fracture); Hank escaped with a sore knee.

COMMENTARY: Though quirk saw that Frank and Hank popped off at essentially the same time and smacked each other ardently, the mishap was avoidable. Overcrowding is hateful at many indoor climbing facilities, especially during peak hours. Most gyms feature routes that crisscross other routes, a fact that needs to be taken into consideration.

PREVENTION: On crisscrossing routes (or on routes that brush shoulders with other routes), wait until the first party has finished the lead and pulled the rope through before you start up. This is not so crucial on vertical or low-angle toprope routes—though even then you don't want to climb on someone else's hip—but on lead climbs and overhung topropes, where bodies tend to careen off and swoop through the air, you need a clear fly zone to avoid the chance of repeating Frank and Hank's aching adventure. This advice is easier said than done, however, because there are countless possibilities for climber/route entanglement in most gyms, especially when climbers are teeming over the wall like ants. If you were to wait for a completely vacant wall, you'd likely still be waiting at closing time. Oftentimes, for instance, a host of routes will finish at the same anchor, and people are jostling and queuing up to climb each of the routes. If one of the routes is grim and someone is working it, you could be waiting for fifteen minutes or more. A method I've seen used here (as long as the routes don't actually crisscross and there's no chance of flying off and clashing in midair) is for climbers to proceed even if someone else is grappling toward the same anchor. Whoever arrives first clips the anchor, lowers off and quickly pulls the rope. If the second climber can't hang and wait, she'll do the last moves up to the anchor and downclimb or drop to the last protection point—usually only a few feet below. A vigilant belayer is necessary for this last procedure. Always think twice before putting yourself in a situation where a fall may result in a collision.

# 40

# RUNNING THE ROPE IN TUOLUMNE MEADOWS

*Ginny's gain is Vinny's pain*

Vinny and Ginny were attempting a new route on a remote dome in Tuolumne Meadows. In theory, the line would follow a 300-foot, left-facing open book. However, because the book started perhaps fifty feet off the deck, the duo was forced to climb up on sparse face holds to reach it. Ginny started leading up the 70-degree slab and sank two bolts, one twenty feet up, and the other about twenty feet farther. At that point the holds thinned appreciably and Ginny found she could only advance by moving up and left—not right, which was ultimately the direction she needed to go to reach the book.

After several falls, she managed the crux and sank a third bolt while balanced on a wee foothold. From there a thin flake led right fifteen feet to the start of the book, but the first few moves looked bleak, and Ginny took several short whippers before gaining the better part of the flake and, in turn, a 5.9 hand crack in the book. Concerned about rope drag, Ginny ran the rope up the book twenty feet before slotting her first nut. Seventy feet higher she reached a stance and rigged a belay. Vinny followed.

Vinny aced the lower slab and now stood at the wee foothold where Ginny had placed the third bolt to protect the barren face moves that traversed to the book.

Vinny unclipped the bolt, chalked his puissant mitts, cast off—and immediately fell. Owing to the steepness of the wall, he pendulumed hard as a wrecking ball into the dihedral, chipping a bone in his elbow. His bum arm hanging at his side, Vinny was incapable of following the remainder of the pitch, obliging Ginny to undertake elaborate rope shenanigans in order to lower Vinny safely to the deck.

COMMENTARY: A protection bolt is commonly placed just before grim face climbing. On a traverse, this is Fat City for the leader, but it sets the second up for a swing if he or she pings on the very moves the bolt was meant to protect.

PREVENTION: Before trying the traverse, Vinny ideally should have rigged a backrope belay to protect the possibility of a pendulum fall. However, this would require a third member of the party to belay the backrope from the ground, and Ginny and Vinny had no such third member. Hence, considering the circumstances, it would have been better for Vinny to keep the rope clipped to the last bolt before the traverse. This way, if he fell while making the moves, he would swing back into open space instead of toward the dihedral. Once he established himself in the corner, he would then set up an anchor, tie off, and pull the end of the rope through, then tie back in. This is elaborate and costs a piece of gear (usually just a biner), but it's better than a chipped bone.

# 41

# LIGHTNING STRIKES THE ARROWHEAD

*Haste wastes Nate's hands*

Dewey and Nate were finishing the classic *Arrowhead Arete* in Yosemite Valley when the skies clouded over and thunder rumbled forth. By the time Dewey had led the last pitch, rain fell in sheets and lightning blasted the main wall some fifty feet away. From the top of the climb, the route traversed a thin arete (the "arrowhead") which dropped breathlessly away on both sides and eventually gained the main wall. However, for reasons unknown to Dewey and Nate, lightning kept dashing the juncture of the arete with the main wall; so, rather than walk straight into a forked shaft of lightning, Dewey decided to rappel directly left off the arete into a boulder-chocked gully that served as the normal descent route. Nate suggested waiting out the storm rather than committing to an uncertain rappel, but Dewey would hear none of this and proceeded to wrap a sling around a stunted tree, rig the rope to it, and toss the line into the descent gully.

Owing to the pounding rain, visibility was poor, so Dewey attached a prusik to one strand of the rappel rope to "safeguard" his descent. He realized too late that he'd forgotten to tie a knot in the ends of the doubled rope; he also realized too late that the ends of the rope were uneven, and when the short end passed through his figure-8, his weight naturally transfered to the long end and caused the rope to whiz through the anchor. Down toward the gully pitched Dewey.

Nate, a born fool but a natural hero, lunged for the whizzing rope in an attempt to grab it. He badly burned his hands before a kink in the line somehow entangled in the anchor sling and girth-hitched the whole mess around the tree. Dewey shock-loaded onto the jammed line, but luckily his prusik grabbed the single strand it was attached to, saving him from serious injury or possibly death. With the extra distance gained in his fall, Dewey (remarkably unscathed) was able to swing into the gully, secure himself, and free the rope for Nate to rappel on. Nate, however, was incapacitated with his badly burned hands, and even if he hadn't been, he couldn't have rappelled into the gully because the rope was too short, when doubled, to reach safe ground. Because they needed the rope to complete the remainder of the descent, tying the rope off and rapping the single line was not an option either.

After waiting out the storm, Dewey grappled up the descent gully, scampered along the arrowhead arete, and made his way back to Nate, who kicked him repeatedly in the shins before demanding that Dewey belay him across to the main wall and then follow. From there, Nate insisted that the crestfallen Dewey lower him down the rest of the descent.

COMMENTARY: It is academic to say the pair should have waited out the storm and descended only when they could do so by the normal route or made sure their rappel into the gully was possible on one doubled rope. However, this judgment ignores the basic human instinct to flee sizzling shafts of lightning that are striking a mere stone's throw away.

PREVENTION: A rappeller should always tie a thick "stopper" knot in the end of the rope unless he or she can visually verify that the line is either on the ground or ends, with slack to spare, on a safe place large enough to ensure that rappelling off the end of the rope is virtually impossible. During multiple rappels it is always standard practice to tie a knot in the end of the rope, regardless of whether you're rapping to a hanging stance or onto a gigantic ledge. Rockfall (sometimes dislodged by their own rappel ropes!) has been known to knock rappellers out cold, and more than one has been saved by the knot at rope's end. In the case of Dewey and Nate, they ultimately broke one important rule: never tackle a multipitch route with only one rope. Two standard-length ropes would have made their rappel into the descent gully a straightforward affair.

# 42

# BULLY'S COMEUPPANCE

*Rediscovering the karma connection*

Dan and Jim drove out to Joshua Tree, intending to practice crack climbing on the many monzonite domes. Both climbers worked at a backpacking adventure retailer in Los Angeles. Neither had roped up together prior to this trip.

At "The Tree," they found the popular sites a veritable ant farm of climbers, so at Dan's urging, the duo escaped to an area known as The Hall of Horrors, a grouping of smallish cliffs with a mess of brief, albeit classic, crack climbs. Surprisingly, they found the area all to themselves. Dan, a rash, self-proclaimed crack champion and veteran of many Yosemite summers, wanted to climb a rugged (5.10d) thin crack called *It*. Jim, keen but inexperienced, favored a more reasonable (5.7) hand crack called *That*. Both *It* and *That* began atop a large block approached via a fifty-foot 5.5 chimney.

Undecided, the duo scaled the chimney to the top of the block, agreeing to pick the route following a visual inspection. The ledge was flat and spacious, so Dan and Jim unroped and moved toward the main wall and the two cracks, one mean *(It)*, one cordial *(That)*. *It* appeared shallow, unprotected, and grainy. *That* looked like locker jamming all the way, though the route passed through a pesky bulge after 30 feet. Dan declared they would first trot up *It*, then Jim could drop back down on a toprope and jam up *That*, if he so desired.

Jim didn't fancy the plan, chiefly because he had never climbed a 5.10 crack. *It* was slanting and unprotected and he feared taking a treacherous pendulum whipper. On top of all that, and lastly, because he was not given to taking direct orders from anyone. Dan and Jim argued. Presently Dan fell into a rage and, in a sovereign act of stupidity, grabbed the rope and pitched it off the ledge, declaring that if Jim wanted to climb *That*, he could follow him up—solo. Otherwise Jim could kick back on the ledge, dry up, and blow away for all Dan cared.

Still furious, Dan chalked up and commenced motoring up the bottlenecked jams of *That*. Jim looked on, dumbfounded. Three moves off the ledge, Dan's foot unexpectedly blew off a grainy foothold and he caught himself only because, in plummeting, his left hand lodged in a bottleneck tight as a fly in amber. Dan reset his boots (which were only five feet above the ledge), but for his best efforts he could not free his lodged hand. He begged and apologized and finally wept openly until Dan hunkered beneath him to provide support. With Dan's boots treading variously on Jim's shoulders and head, Dan was eventually able to free his hand, and in a jump/catch effort, he returned to the sanctuary of the ledge. Dan's hand, however, quickly swelled to the diameter of a small dog—and they had no rope. They did have hardware, and by placing assorted pro and protecting himself with slings, Jim was able to downclimb the 5.5 chimney, fetch the rope, and reclimb the chimney to the ledge. The pair then rappelled to the deck.

COMMENTARY: Beginning and intermediate climbers are well served to climb with more experienced leaders whenever possible. Studying a master's technique, to say nothing of following a route more difficult than one could possibly lead, can quickly steepen your learning curve. The trouble is when the disparity between the expert and the second is somewhat the difference between a Turbo Porsche and a Geo, and when said expert is locked into "crank" mode. Here, the second is reduced to a belay slave, will likely get yarded up a climb far beyond his/her ability and will have to like it. Beware of the expert who shows up at the cliffside alone and, grinning like a jackal, invites you along for the ride.

PREVENTION: It is said that friendship is the ventilation of the soul, but you would do well to shutter yourself against the likes of Dan. Even on the most casual climbs, pick your partners wisely.

# 43

# LOST LINE

*What we've got here is a failure to communicate*

Chuck and Antoine had each climbed El Capitan over a dozen times, but neither hardman had bagged the sweeping, shit-rotten *North America Wall*, which at the time of the first ascent (1964) was hailed as the world's most difficult aid climb. Now, twenty years later, Chuck and Antoine were ready to take a shot at glory. Hoping to hammer well up the wall on the first day, the party fixed the initial four pitches—a standard practice—up to Mazatlan Ledge. During fixing, they hauled their bag along and left it on the ledge. The first two fixed lines were "junk" cords they would drop when they went for it; the third and fourth fixed ropes were the duo's haul line and lead rope.

On the fateful morning, the climbers were joined by a friend who was to recover the first and second fixed ropes once they were dropped. Chuck started jugging the fixed lines, shooting skyward like a cruise missile; Antoine followed. At the top of the first line, Antoine changed over to the second line, dropping the first line. The friend retrieved and coiled it presently. At the top of the second line, Antoine switched over to the third line and dropped the second. It, too, was fetched and coiled.

At the top of the third line, Chuck, already on Mazatlan Ledge, yelled down for Antoine to "get the friggin' lead out." A harried Antoine changed over to the fourth and last fixed line—and dropped the third. The friend on the ground yelled up, wondering why the hell Antoine had pitched one of his climbing ropes. Indeed,

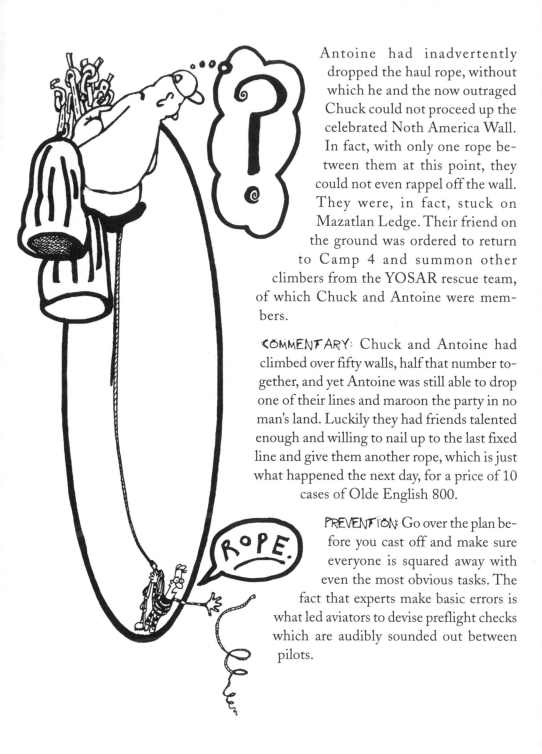

Antoine had inadvertently dropped the haul rope, without which he and the now outraged Chuck could not proceed up the celebrated Noth America Wall. In fact, with only one rope between them at this point, they could not even rappel off the wall. They were, in fact, stuck on Mazatlan Ledge. Their friend on the ground was ordered to return to Camp 4 and summon other climbers from the YOSAR rescue team, of which Chuck and Antoine were members.

COMMENTARY: Chuck and Antoine had climbed over fifty walls, half that number together, and yet Antoine was still able to drop one of their lines and maroon the party in no man's land. Luckily they had friends talented enough and willing to nail up to the last fixed line and give them another rope, which is just what happened the next day, for a price of 10 cases of Olde English 800.

PREVENTION: Go over the plan before you cast off and make sure everyone is squared away with even the most obvious tasks. The fact that experts make basic errors is what led aviators to devise preflight checks which are audibly sounded out between pilots.

# 44

# MISHAP AT MATTRESS QUARRY

*Skydiving into the slag heap*

Sid and Timothy were attempting a new face climb on the scaly ramparts of Mattress Quarry, a squat, repulsive, trash-strewn quarry of lousy rock and ripe fecal matter near the popular bouldering area of Mount Rubidoux, California. After plowing up a precipitous slag heap, Sid established an anchor at the base of the steep, albeit foul, sixty-foot face; Timothy commenced cranking up on a succession of pliable edges and suspicious carbuncles, announcing to the fretting Sid his design to gain a big chickenhead some twenty feet up before sinking the first protection bolt. A suave climber, though systematically moronic, Timothy had no sooner highstepped onto the chickenhead than it popped. He plunged down and landed squarely on Sid's right shoulder, then ricocheted off and jangled another twenty feet down the dreadful slag heap before grinding to a stop.

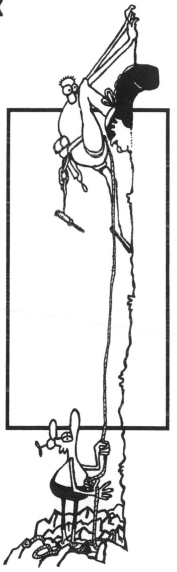

COMMENTARY: Sid suffered a second-degree shoulder separation that later required surgery; Timothy broke two fingers and dislocated his ankle. Ironically, the pair originally decided to attempt to establish the climb in the "old style"—from the ground up—because the top of the crag was so stacked with tottering blocks and detritus they judged it too dangerous to rap from the top and install the much-needed protection bolts.

PREVENTION: Though the fall might have been unavoidable, at the very least Sid should have positioned his belay so Timothy was not clawing up unprotected ground directly over his bean. It is common on routes featuring loose rock for the belayer to take cover and stand—sometimes even crouched or hunkered down—out of the direct line of fire. The same holds true when belaying someone running the rope out directly off the deck. I think somewhere in Sid's star-crossed mind he felt his position might serve as a nominal spot if his buddy Timothy pinged before setting the first bolt. This might have worked for the first body length or so, but after the leader's feet are eight to ten feet off the ground, Hulk Hogan himself could do little to arrest the falling leader. I figure that after two body lengths at the very most (more like one body length if the wall is steep), the leader's on his own.

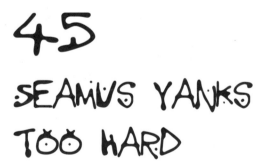

# 45

# SEAMUS YANKS TOO HARD

*Jules "barked like a dog"*

Jules, a dour and hatchet-faced Hungarian, was hanging in slings below pitch four—a long, A3 dihedral—on the *Kor Route*, Gold Wall, Yosemite. His partner, Seamus, a young and nervous Irishman, was perhaps fifteen feet up the pitch when his trail line entangled inside a small flake on the otherwise bald face left of the dihedral. Gentle tugging on the line only further lodged it, whence the restless Seamus grabbed the rope with both hands and yarded with all his might, peeling the flake off the wall.

Jules scarcely had time to duck before the flake, roughly the size of Ulster, bashed straight onto his noggin. Fortunately, Jules was wearing a helmet, which was "split like a goat's hoof" by the impact. The violent blow opened up a slight but bloody gash on Jules's scalp and knocked him so loopy that for half an hour he "barked like a dog" (according to Seamus). Seamus was able to down-clip back to the belay, tend his partner's wound, and after the yelping had tailed off, affect a descent.

COMMENTARY: Believe it: even on such well-traveled routes as those found on the Gold Wall there is oftentimes some loose rock on hand, particularly off to the side of the actual climbing. When the trail rope hangs up it's most everyone's impulse to try and yank it free if at all possible. This tactic is good for one of three results: freeing the line (unlikely); lodging the rope even worse (sometimes cutting and often abrading it); or, in the sad case of Jules and Seamus, yarding off whatever the rope is hung up on and unloading it on your helpless partner.

PREVENTION: Vigilance is required to avoid any rock that looks even remotely suspect, no matter how many ascents the route has enjoyed. And the business of trying to yank free a stuck line kinked behind an obviously loose flake is patently rash, especially when the belayer is lashed in the direct line of fire. It would have been much saner for Seamus to have lowered down on the lead rope, swung or even pulled himself over on the stuck line and taken it from there . . . gingerly. If there was ever an endorsement for wearing a hard hat on walls (now standard practice), this mishap is surely it.

# 46

# RALPH'S RUGGED RAP

*He slid down the line like a bead on a string*

Ralph had joined a group of twenty daredevils in Yosemite Valley with the goal of rappelling the great face of El Capitan. Half a dozen 600-foot, 7/16-inch diameter ropes had been strung down the chillingly steep Southeast Face, somewhere in the vicinity of the Dawn Wall. Using a caver's rappelling device, which can accommodate up to six brakebars, Ralph had descended approximately 400 feet when he lost control of his rappel and slid down the line like a bead on a string, screaming 200 feet till he wrenched to a stop at the next anchor.

COMMENTARY: Some years ago I broke the world's record for continuous rappel—twice. The first time was down Angel Falls in Venezuela, with Jim Bridwell. The second was a 3,000-foot rap from a helicopter. I got pressed into doing the rappel when the stuntman, now deceased, refused to do the gag and I (the lowly writer for the now-defunct TV show that was filming the rappel) was forced into it by default. From these two experiences I can appreciate both the goofball attraction and the real danger of executing huge rappels. I found it senseless and dangerous even when paid a small fortune to do it—and yet I did it anyway, so I'm standing in quicksand when knocking the notion. But the fact is, most experienced climbers avoid all but the most straightforward or obligatory rappels. To go out and rappel for the sport of it, especially down something as titanic as the face of El Capitan, is perhaps no more pointless than climbing up the same cliff, but it's a dangerous procedure that novices can get lured into trying by the seeming ease of executing a shorter rappel. Regardless of what I may think, however, parties periodically mount expeditions to rappel the great faces of Yosemite and other illustrious areas.

PREVENTION: There are many factors involved in safely accomplishing a long rappel. The weight of the rope is usually in excess of a hundred pounds, which can put so much friction on the brake/rappel device that descent is slow and often laborious, even with minimal brakebars. The farther down you descend, there is less weight (and therefore less friction) on the rappel device. For this reason, it is necessary to occasionally stop and add more brakebars to compensate for the decreased friction on the rappel device. This can get complicated, especially when the rappeller is left to heft, say, fifty pounds of rope up, unhook from and rearrange his descending device, and then carry on. Many times a hauling system is required: you first secure yourself to the rope; rig a system to haul up the rope below; anchor it above your rappelling system, so the weight of the rope is off your descender; rerig your descender; then break down the hauling system and carry on. This procedure is usually where sport rappellers go wrong. It's a fact that few sport rappellers are experienced climbers. Virtually none have the required big-wall experience to safely and efficiently handle the complicated rope-hauling system; it simply confounds them, especially when dangling in an exposed environment that is mind-boggling even to seasoned wall rats. For my money, sport rappellers are better off dinking around on Swan Slab or similar small outcrops. The face of a big wall is no place for a novice—period. And if an experienced climber/rappeller wants to get into the perilous business of huge rappels, it's best to ease into the undertaking—very slowly.

# 47

# 'SUGAR' LOST HER LOAD

*Roland should have known*

Roland was grunting up the 110-degree nothingness of a popular sport route at Red Rocks in Nevada. Gina belayed, the line running out of a rope bag, through her belay device, and up to Roland, who, upon gaining a two-bolt anchor at the top of the climb, leaned back and yelled, "Take, Sugar . . .".

Gina began lowering Roland down the cliffside. Because the corn-fed Roland outweighed Gina by seventy-five pounds, and because he was hanging free from the overhanging wall for the duration of his descent, Gina was forced to work overtime to control Roland's speed. Because she was concentrating so hard on this task, she remained oblivious to the shocking fact that, as Roland was nearing the touchdown, the end of the line had snaked out of the rope bag and there wasn't enough slack left to get Roland all the way down. In a flash, the end slipped through Gina's belay device—and the hapless Roland augered straight into the deck from fifteen feet up, cracking both heels upon impact.

COMMENTARY: Roland later told me that since his lead rope was 200 feet long, he "thought" it sufficient to lower him off the 108-foot climb. This very accident, in one form or another, is happening all too frequently these days at sport-climbing areas.

PREVENTION: The first mistake Roland made was to not recognize the fact that his single rope did not provide sufficient slack for him to be lowered all the way to the ground from the belay station. Second, before he started up the route he should have flaked the cord onto the ground (which was a flat rock slab) so Gina could see how much—or how little—rope remained as she lowered him. The fact that the belayer (Gina) was not tied into the other end of the rope was also a critical oversight, because that practice would have prevented this mishap. Add to this growing list of oversights the fact that Gina had not taken notice of the rope's halfway mark, which must have passed through her hands just as Roland neared the top of the route; seeing said halfway mark should have set off alarms in Gina's head, because obviously, if the rope is more than halfway out and the climber is not yet at the top of the route, there will not be enough rope left to lower said climber from the anchor. (If for some reason the rope's halfway point wasn't marked at all, this is another critical oversight, because all ropes should be marked to help prevent accidents such as this.)

When the belayer realizes that there isn't enough rope to safely lower the climber, an alternative method of descent must be enacted, such as hauling up a second line and rappelling to the ground. This accident was particularly embarrassing and painful for an experienced climber like Roland, since it was completely avoidable if only he and Sugar had followed standard procedures.

# 48

# NIGHTMARE ON SEA OF DREAMS

*Their teeth chattered like those wind-up dentures*

John and Don, both experienced wall climbers, had spent five days tapping up the *Sea of Dreams* on El Capitan, renowned as one of the most technically demanding rock climbs in the world. They reached a height of 2,000 feet when heavy weather set in. As bad luck would have it, their hanging bivouac was positioned beneath a shallow open book, where the converging planes of rock formed a funnel of sorts. As the rain increased, an absolute torrent poured down the funnel and directly onto John and Don. (Don later commented that they might have weathered the storm had high winds not blown away their portaledge's rainfly when John was in the process of securing it.)

Unprotected from the gusher, both climbers were quickly soaked and soon thereafter grew hypothermic. When the rain passed, the weather remained cool and

gusty; John and Don were wracked with convulsive shivers. A rescue was finally arranged: climbers lowered down from the top of El Cap with warm liquids and dry clothes and, after some semblance of alertness and energy had returned to the withered duo, the rescuers assisted them on the 600-foot jumar to the rim.

COMMENTARY: I could fill 200 pages with similar stories about climbers getting caught in storms and suffering epics at the very least—and, at the very worst, death. Instead of the many available examples, I've chosen to offer up only this one rather typical (but involved) case study and comment from there. Lengthy discussion of individual instances is more interesting than instructional because it basically boils down to one thing: the climbing team found themselves unprepared for a bad turn of weather and their situation quickly became life threatening.

If we consider Yosemite Valley a metaphor for all so-called fair-weather climbing areas, we can draw several important conclusions. First, regardless of how sunny the valley (or any fair-weather locale) usually is during summer months, freak thundershowers can and do strike. For instance, I once hiked up to Mount Watkins with two other climbers, heart set on bagging the 3,000-foot regular route. But mid-July heat welled off the great ivory face so fiendishly that we could barely touch the rock, and climbing was out of the question. About six years later I returned—also in mid-July—with Jim Bridwell and Kim Schmitz, this time to attempt a new route up the same wall. The weather was perfect. We had fixed two pitches when suddenly it started raining; then it started storming; and finally, about three that morning, I would have sworn we were in Borneo during the monsoon. We huddled under the lee of a huge boulder and gazed up in awe at veritable cresting waves rolling down the face, the whole scene highlighted in brilliant moonlight. Though such storms are rare in mid-July, they *do* happen, and if you don't come prepared for them you might just get caught with your pants down.

Another factor in fair weather areas is that "fair" generally refers to a certain window of time, usually two to three months during the summer, during which the weather is typically benign. Once you start working on the sills of this window, the chances of getting caught in the last—or the first—winter storm increase dramatically. About a decade ago a Japanese team of three was topping out on the *Nose* in late August when a cold front moved in and a foot of snow fell overnight. The very next morning rescuers were helicoptored to the summit of El Cap; when they rapped down, they found the Japanese trio lashed to the final belay, entombed in a giant icicle. Rangers from Rocky Mountain National Park to the Canadian Rockies all cite the disastrous refrains they so frequently hear from visiting climbers: "I'd always heard the weather was good this time of year . . ." or "I thought it was always sunny in California . . .".

Back in the '70s, wall climbers made a rule of always carrying with them some form of rain protection, even if it was just a meager plastic trash bag, tube tent, or waterproof ground cloth—*anything* that would keep them from getting soaked to the bone was better than nothing. This, coupled with some form of insulation—a thick pile coat, for instance—will allow a climber to weather almost any rainstorm and recover enough to carry on or retreat. Snow is a different matter altogether and may require additional gear.

PROTECTION: The best protection is to avoid bad weather in the first place. Weather forecasting has come so far in the last decade that five-day forecasts are now between sixty and seventy percent accurate. Two-day forecasts are ninety percent accurate. Of the many people who have been rescued from storms, the majority never checked the weather report, and if they did, they came unprepared regardless.

Climbing a big wall is hard work, particularly a long nail-up that can entail a week on the stone and a haulbag weighing 100 pounds. The urge to shave off every ounce of weight is strong, but if you leave out the rain gear you might regret it or pay for it with your life. Remember, Yosemite is an aberration as far as rescues go—there is a world-class rescue team on standby, and helicopters are available at a moment's notice. However, none of this changes the fact that on longer climbs bad weather is a formidable threat because quick descent is so difficult, and the bulk of long climbs are not in yelling distance of help. Always carry adequate rain gear and warm clothes. Period.

# 49

# DOWNWARD BOUND

*The day the slings gave way*

G and B, two San Francisco climbers both with five years experience, had just completed an ascent of *Stone Groove*, a thin, tricky 5.10 crack near the Cookie Cliff in Yosemite. The "Groove" is actually a first-pitch variation of a longer route; it ends at a belay shared by both routes. Since the longer route is a confirmed pile, it sees little traffic while the popular *Groove* typically enjoys several ascents a day during the Valley's peak months. Teams simply bag the ninety-foot-long Groove pitch and rap off at the first belay.

When B and G reached the above-mentioned belay, they found hunkered back in a V-shaped alcove several slings that were threaded through two fixed angles (over the years the nature of this belay/rap anchor has changed many times). G threaded the rope through the slings, evened up the ends of the rope, and pitched them off for the short rappel to the deck. B went first. As G followed, B remembers hearing a telltale, "Christ, almighty."

Looking up, he saw G torpedoing down toward the ground from a height of twenty-five feet. SLAM, G impacted the ground right next to B and proceeded to cartwheel an additional thirty feet down the slope at the base of the wall. As a result of this fall, G sustained fractures to both legs and bad lacerations all over his body.

COMMENTARY: Inspection later that afternoon showed that the two slings which were fitted through the fixed pegs were stiff and burned (from previous teams pulling their lines through) and had simply blown under G's body weight. Understand that it is not unusual for popular "traditional" climbs to feature a rappel off something other than a sport-climbing anchor. On many such climbs, it doesn't matter if the anchor be bolts or pins or both—the lowering point is usually a ratty braid of old one-inch tubular nylon slings. Because untold ropes have already been yanked through the braid, the slings are likely badly burned. Exposure to U.V. rays (sunlight) can also greatly weaken a sling or runner, no matter if it's made of nylon, Spectra, or whatever.

PREVENTION: Recent tests show that when an anchor has more than five slings, even when the slings are in very poor condition, the chances are remote that body weight will cause all the slings to fail. That's reassuring to know. But when there is any doubt whatsoever, I personally thread a new sling through the anchor and call it good—because I know it is. Many climbers have needlessly died trying to save a piece of equipment. And remember, just because the sling or slings are good doesn't mean the anchor is. Both the anchor AND the rigging must check out.

# 50

# RED ALERT!

*Natasha crashes like Sputnik*

A group of seven Russian émigrés from a local community college climbing club had strung a toprope on the Potato Wall (about fity feet high) at Stoney Point, a popular bouldering and practice area in Chatsworth, California. The 9 mm rope was secured on top by slings looped around large blocks. Outing leaders Vladamir Vodkov and Boris Alcoholove had extended the slings a foot or so over the lip so that the anchor point allowed the rope to run smoothly, rather than over the edge. All told, the toprope setup was almost letter perfect. Almost . . . .

Natasha Smirnov started up the 5.7 face; Petra Dipsomanov, lashed taut to a ground anchor, belayed. Natasha clawed about six feet up the climb and fell off. The rope stretched and she smacked a boulder at the base, tweaking both ankles.

**COMMENTARY:** 9 mm lead ropes are poor for toproping because they stretch so much, especially in a case like this where over 100 feet of line is out. Add the flex in any system and Natasha Smirnov didn't have a chance.

**PREVENTION:** This short episode is included because of how frequently it happens. There are several credible manuals on toproping procedure (including *Toproping* by S. Peter Lewis, Falcon Publishing, 1998), but we can mention here a few key elements. First, use an 11 mm rope whenever possible. An 11 mm line stretches less than a 9 mm line. Some toproping enthusiasts use static ropes, which eliminate virtually all stretch. Knowing that all lead ropes stretch when fallen upon, make certain to snug the cord somewhat tight for that first ten or fifteen feet, where a groundfall is possible. The belayer should be taut to the anchor to eliminate the possibility that body movement will put extra slack in the system and allow the toproped climber to hit the ground if they fall off down low.

# 51

# SHIVERING ON THE SPIRE

*"The rope slid through the anchors!"*

Andy had been climbing for two years when he roped his dad Amos into joining him for a day's cragging in the illustrious Black Hills of South Dakota. Once there, the duo's mood was dampened when they found an icy drizzle bleeding through fog thick as that on an English moor. Despite the weather, Andy decided to show Pop how it was done; scaling back his original ambitions, he decided to scale *Hrum Hroom*, a dicey 5.7 face job that gained the top of a spire so steep and skinny that a rappel was the only way off.

Amos, a stout, suspicious man whose climbing experience consisted of two toprope outings, anchored off and belayed the intrepid fruit of his loins up the bolted lower face, which Andy dispelled with a vigor reserved for those who perform in front of their parents. Feeling solid despite a veneer of ice water running over the wall, Andy forged higher into the fog. Several feet below the top, Andy couldn't be bothered to sling an obvious flake for protection and instead scampered for the slender summit, where he attached himself to the anchor chain, untied from the rope and ran it through the rings, preparing to rappel to the ground and then belay his dad on toprope.

Suddenly, Andy decided on a whim that he was going to miss a splendid photo opportunity—that of his pop emerging from an ocean of fog, clawing up the sodden cobbles to the crown—if he didn't belay from above and have his camera ready. He instructed Amos to tie the camera onto one end of the doubled rope. Amos did as much and Andy hauled up his photographic equipment. The camera now in hand, Andy untied it from the rope, which he unclasped for the briefest second—just enough time for the line to snake through the anchor chains and snag on the last bolt, thirty feet of drenched 5.7 climbing below, some seventy-five feet off the deck.

Trying to downclimb the face—sans rope—was not an option. Neither was seeking help from other climbers, as Amos and Andy had the rainy crag all to themselves. Amos had no choice but to drive into town and call his other son, who gathered his climbing gear and immediately set off from Rapid City, an hour's drive away. Meanwhile, the drizzle increased to a downpour. Stranded on the puny, rounded, exposed and storm-swept summit, clad only in jeans and a cotton shirt, Andy began shaking as though he had dengue fever and was more dead than alive when his brother (Amos Jr.) finally grappled to his aid, two hours later.

COMMENTARY: Dropping ropes is a common occurrence, but most such scenarios don't punish the victim as thoroughly as this case did Andy. But Andy was lucky: he escaped in one piece because help could be summoned. Drop your line when there is nobody around to help, and you're finished.

PREVENTION: Dress for the weather (don't wear jeans and a T-shirt in the rain). Make sure the rope is anchored off at all times. Period. Sounds simple—and it is.

So long as you never break this rule, you can never drop the rope. Note that when one is handling the line—when it is not tied off—bad things can happen. The case to be avoided at all costs is when the only thing keeping the rope in your possession is your hands. If for some unforeseen reason this is unavoidable, at least wrap the line around your leg several times so if the rope somehow gets away, it won't fall into the void. When untying to thread the rope through an anchor, simply clip a bight of rope to a biner on your harness before you begin the process.

# 52

# ASTEROIDS FLY ON ASTROMAN

*Ned gets nailed upside the head*

Ned and Sam were honed up and ambitious. As one testpiece after another fell beneath their boots, anything seemed possible. Naturally, they wished upon a star: Yosemite's glorious *Astroman*, the original free wall and one of the world's premier trad routes. They had to bag it.

So it was that early one morning Ned and Sam trudged up to the East Face of Washington Column, girded their loins, clawed the ground and tied in for *Astroman*. Feeling confident, Ned stormed up the first pitch on lead. Supernaturally psyched and blasting along, soon he was 60 feet out with no gear in yet. Suddenly, from far above, the dreadful words rang out— "HAULBAG!"

Ned reflexively pasted himself into the corner, glanced up, and, the way he tells it, "saw this pig flying toward me." The chances were one in a million that a haulbag jettisoned from hundreds of feet above would find its mark on Ned's cringing frame, but to his horror and amazement, the pig continued to spin straight toward him. It smashed into the dihedral just above, smacked him upside the head as it tore past, then shot into the deck and exploded at Sam's feet.

Astonishingly, Ned held on to the wall and didn't follow the pig into the ground. He claims that the glancing blow did, however, cause "an adrenaline rush better than any speed-ball." He and Sam managed to finish the pitch and continue the climb. Several leads later they met the varlet who had dropped the haulbag, to whom Ned directed a few choice words. Then he and Sam chugged on to glory.

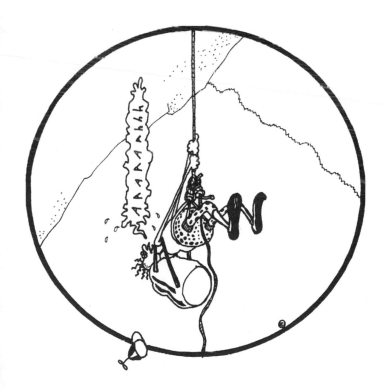

COMMENTARY: The haulbag belonged to a team (Zeke and Gino) rapping off an aid attempt on *Astroman*. Here's what happened: Zeke had tied two ropes together to make a long, single-rope rappel. His partner, Gino, was going to pull the ropes back up, thread as normal and do two raps to join Zeke. The reason Zeke was doing the long rappel was because he was rapping with the haulbag and he wanted to save time and hassle. He put the bag on his back and took off.

When he gained the knot that connected the two ropes, he had no clue how to properly pass the knot through his rappel device. He was dangling and spinning in midair, and the weight of the bag began to pull him over backwards. Futilely he tried to take himself off rappel by putting his weight on one jumar above the knot, but soon he found himself hanging dead upside down with no way to right himself. Virtually stuck in this manner, he had little choice but to just let the bag go.

PREVENTION: Knot passes and rappelling with a haulbag are complicated procedures made easier if you know exactly what you are doing and—of equal importance—have practiced these techniques in controlled situations. Neither technique should be attempted for the first time on a Yosemite big wall. Various illustrations are needed to properly explain these techniques. Refer to a manual to get the basics or better yet, take a seminar and learn the techniques under expert supervision.

# 53

# HELL IN ELDORADO

*Violet needed elbow room*

Charley had been climbing for twenty years and thought he had seen it all—till he and his girlfriend Violet tried to tackle *Washington Irving* (5.7) in Eldorado Canyon near Boulder, Colorado, one of America's favorite recreational crags. Violet had been climbing for three seasons, had followed Charley up many climbs, could clean gear quickly and was gaining skill in placing pro, rigging belays, etc. She had also recently begun charging out on the sharp end, having just completed a week-long Learning to Lead seminar in nearby Estes Park. According to boyfriend Charley, her approach to leading was "careful and systematic, with safety remaining her primary concern." Indeed, she had already led the first pitch of *Washington Irving* several days before and wanted to repeat the lead for practice; such was the state of things when Violet drew a deep breath and headed up the climb again. Charley belayed.

Violet made facile progress up the taxing fissure, placing sound gear at regular intervals. Twenty feet off the deck she slotted a bomber hex and climbed smoothly through the crux to a good rest. Standing on distinguished holds, arm-barring with her left arm, she placed another nut, clipped in and prepared to move on.

To her surprise, however, she found her left arm was now snugly lodged in the crack. Apparently, while placing the pro, she had allowed her elbow to take the weight of the jam, and now the limb was stuck fast as a turd in a drainpipe. Violet huffed. Violet puffed. Violet farted sonorously. But the limb wouldn't budge.

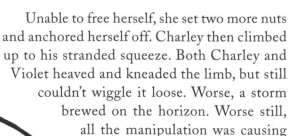

Unable to free herself, she set two more nuts and anchored herself off. Charley then climbed up to his stranded squeeze. Both Charley and Violet heaved and kneaded the limb, but still couldn't wiggle it loose. Worse, a storm brewed on the horizon. Worse still, all the manipulation was causing Violet's limb to swell, getting it more stuck. The pain was beginning to count, and Violet was getting desperate.

Charley decided to rap off and go fetch help. He had no sooner touched down when a light went on in Violet's head. It was her habit to carry a tube of Blistex in her sport top ("Right in one of my favorite little spots," according to Charley). Violet pulled out the Blistex and squirted same liberally into the crack around her lodged elbow. Now greased as a hog on a spit, a little wiggling freed Violet's appendage.

COMMENTARY: The ability to execute a self-rescue should be at the top of every climber's skill list. Barring injuries that require immediate attention, don't give up on your own rescue until you have exercised all the alternatives. The key, as always, is to avoid hysteria—which is a wonderfully easy thing to say sitting here at my computer, nursing a cigar, strains of "South Pacific" lofting from my stereo. Unfortunately, it's never that easy out in the real world, strapped to a real cliff. But if you can retain some small objectivity, obscure solutions may present themselves.

PREVENTION: Hands, feet, arms, and knees getting stuck in cracks is not unheard of and occurs for the same reason that a nut gets fixed: a larger object (an elbow, in this case) is weighted, shifts down into a constriction and gets stuck. If you feel your limb being keyed in place when you stick it in a crack, be very cautious with the jam. Though I've never heard of anyone losing a limb that got stuck in a crack, some horrendous epics have resulted from this, so your best insurance is to avoid the circumstances whenever possible.

# 54

# CURLY JOE TAKES A SHORTCUT

*Moe cracks his melon*

Three seasoned Yosemite hardmen (Larry, Moe, and Curly Joe) decided to warm down one day on a moderately hard (5.10c) two-pitch route at the Cookie Cliff. The trio had spent the day at the cliff and had bagged half a dozen top-end routes. All three stooges had scaled numerous big walls and had loafed and climbed for many years in and out of the Valley.

Larry led the first pitch, an indecent thin crack that snaked up the left side of a small pillar and ended on a meager ledge. Moe followed, trailing a second rope to belay Curly Joe. Shortly, all three stooges were huddled on the meager ledge, arguing amongst themselves as to whom would score the next lead (the crux), which traversed left over equivocal horns before finding an off-finger crack that led to a grand ledge and the end of the route. Curly Joe won the honors and ticked the second pitch in five minutes flat. Larry followed flawlessly, commenting to Curly Joe that—given the chance—he (Larry) would have dusted the lead in three minutes.

At the anchor, Larry untied from the rope he'd been belayed on. Then he tied the second rope (the line he'd been trailing) into the anchor, leaving the other end attached to the rear loop on the back of his harness (the loop meant for attaching trail ropes); he deemed this loop of sufficient strength to keep him secured to the anchor and did not bother tying into the designated belay/rappel loop on the front of his harness. He also did not bother to tie in tight to the anchor, but instead left a good loop of slack on the ground so that he could position himself more comfortably on the ledge. Declaring himself ready, he yelled at Moe to begin climbing; the unsuspecting Moe dashed out sideways across the vague knobs, headed for the crack.

But before Moe could get his mitts firmly slotted in the crevice, a knob popped and off he came. Because Larry was not tied in tight to the anchor, the force of the fall jerked him toward the lip of the ledge. The combined weight of himself and Moe then shock-loaded the rope—and the rear loop on Larry's harness immediately ripped out. Larry was no longer attached to the anchor; as a result, Moe was no longer on belay.

Moe found himself hurtling headfirst toward the earth. Because Larry had initially (and luckily) tied the end of the rope off to the anchor when he first reached the ledge, it did arrest Moe's fall when he was still ten feet off the deck; due to rope stretch, however, Moe's melon still managed to smack the ground hard, resulting in a lump the size of a rugby ball. Then the stretch came out of the rope and Moe sprang back up, coming to a stop several feet off the deck.

Larry, meanwhile, was still skydiving. Forty feet from the ground he smashed through the branches of a tree

and decelerated enough so that he was able to stagger away with only a cracked elbow and a medley of heinous abrasions.

Curly Joe rapped down on the free rope to find Moe dazed and dangling ten feet off the deck. An involved sequence of rope shenanigans was then required to lower Moe the rest of the way to the ground.

COMMENTARY: Ace climbers . . . end of the day . . . last route . . . middling difficulty . . . thoughts of a cold beer, vittles, "poon," and Lord knows what else dancing through these young men's heads—clearly, safety was not their primary concern. Beware of circumstances that can allow a cavalier attitude to creep into your day. This incident should have killed both climbers. It demonstrates the price often paid by climbers who try to shortcut a standard safety procedure— properly tying off to an anchor. Moe was innocent because he couldn't have possibly known what was going on; Larry, on the other hand, should have known better than to trust the rear loop on his harness as his one and only physical attachment to the anchor. If you ever anchor off to this loop on the backside of your harness, always back it up to your designated belay/rappel loop on the front of your harness. Curly Joe, who was standing on the ledge watching Larry prepare to belay Moe, should have sounded off when he saw what Larry was up to. When climbers neglect the most basic rules of a safe belay system, it's incredible how often a "fluke" will conspire to make those climbers sorry they ever tied into a rope.

PREVENTION: The standard setup requires: a sound, multicomponent, multidirectional anchor, equalized, with no extension possible if one component should pull when shock-loaded. The belayer should be tied off to the front, not the back, of the harness (or both). There should be no slack in the line between the belayer and the anchor. These are the basics, and are neglected only at one's (and one's partners) imminent peril.

# 55

# INADEQUATE CORDAGE

*Monty's left marooned in high mountain mess*

Monty and Punky both fancied the flaky gray granite and blinding blue sky of California's Sierra Nevada, and often

went climbing on the many splintered crags spilling off Mount Whitney's eastern massif. They returned one day to their favorite butte, a saw toothed 400 footer, and had just polished off a splendid route that followed a hand crack and ended with a seventy-foot, 5.10a lieback summit pitch. When Punky powered up the last few moves to the top, she embarrassingly admitted that, at the last belay, she'd been unable to clean a #3 Camelot Monty had shoved several yards in the back of a flare.

Monty fumed, declaring she'd left him no choice but to rap back to the last belay ledge and fetch the pricey camming unit. He angrily looped the cord round a stunted pine and backpedaled down the wall, angling slightly right to follow the curving summit pitch. There weren't but six inches of slack remaining on the doubled line when Monty's slippers touched down on the small ledge. And when he let go with his brake hand, that last six inches of slack—and the rope itself, now tight as an E-string from his weight—zipped up through his belay/rappel device and TWANGED! up and across the wall to his left, far out of reach.

"Biscuit!" Monty yelled furiously. Had Punky done her job and cleaned the camming device in the first place, Monty raged, he wouldn't have found himself in this blasted fix! As they had only the one line, Punky could only try to pitch an end down and left to Monty. Twenty tries later, she gave up and, on a single rope, rappelled/pendulumed back down to Monty, who ragged on her shamelessly for "causing" the fiasco. Monty spent twenty minutes trying to clean the Camelot, but could not, accusing Punky of fixing the $60 device during her blundering efforts to remove it. Punky informed the vain and gusting Monty that she'd been unable to even *reach* the Camelot since he'd shoved it so deep into the flair that only a silly fool like him, with arms long as rake handles, could even reach it. Shortly the rhubarb lost steam and Monty labored back to the top, sliding a prusik along the line to affect a self-belay.

COMMENTARY: Once Monty decided to rap down and fetch the fixed camming device, every one of his technical decisions was questionable.

PREVENTION: First, climbing a multipitch route with only one rope is a liability. Second, if there was any doubt that there was insufficient line to make the rap on a doubled rope, Monty should have tied himself into the free end and rapped on a single line. Three, rapping down the last pitch of a long route without first tying a knot into the end of the rope is insanity. Again, Monty's safe and sane solution would have been to tie one end of the rope off to the tree, physically tie into the other end, and then rap on a single line. Once on the ledge, Monty could then waste his time trying to clean the nut he fixed (while blaming Punky for same), then Punky could have belayed Monty back to the top on the single line.

# 56

# HERBERT CALLS THE SHOT

*Herbie comes up short*

Herbert (age 40) and his son, Herbie (age 7), hiked up to Suicide Rock at record speed, for Herbert had decided Herbie would lead the classic *Surprise* (5.8) that morning. Though Herbie had been following his dad up climbs since his baby teeth came in, this would be his first experience on the sharp end. Following his dad's instruction, Herbie led up the easy but unprotected 5.2 slab for perhaps 100 feet, then traversed right along a small ledge to the first bolt protecting the 5.8 crux. The bolt, however, proved to be out of Herbie's reach because it had been drilled by a six-foot adult. Unable to clip, stuck 100 feet up a slab sans pro, Herbie stood firm as his dad quickly soloed up to the bolt and straightened things out.

COMMENTARY: Things could have worked out gravely for little Herbie. Had he panicked and pitched off, Herbert would have had little choice but to go behind the shed and blow his own brains out for the stupidity of putting his son on an underprotected lead the first time out.

PREVENTION: No matter how much hard rock you might have followed or toproped, the moment you find yourself out on the sharp end the experience is totally different—even on a benign sport route bolted from bottom to top. The rule of thumb is: for those first dozen or so leads, stick with well-protected routes at a grade you can easily handle. There will be plenty of opportunities to "run the rope" if you stick with climbing. It's madness to begin your leading career on anything but routes affording bomber pro. Some people can never adapt to the special skills required on the sharp end. Better to find out where you stand as a leader by beginning on routes where the penalty for a fall is relatively slight.

# 57

# "HOLY S#%T!"

*Upton goes upside down*

Upton and Hagatha had just finished an ascent of *Tombstone* and were lounging on the wee and airy crown. Rising like a mighty fist, the 150-foot formation features a descent via a formidable free-hanging rappel off the east face, a rappel that novice Hagatha was loathe to perform. Her only rappelling experience was several short raps down practice slabs in the local climbing gymnasium. Not to worry, Upton declared. He would set up the whole business and would go first—to show her how it was done and to instill confidence.

Gazing into the abyss and pondering the boulder-strewn deck far below, Hagatha sensed an epic in the offing and told Upton so. (Hagatha was adept at reading runes, Tarot cards and tea leaves, and when she had a hunch, one could usually take it to the bank.) "Forget that bunkum," Upton laughed. "It's only rappelling. Nothing to it." He'd verbally walk Hagatha down the rope, he said, then they would repair to the local pub for refreshments and eventually slip back to Upton's dump to review several charcoal etchings he'd recently completed.

Upton rigged a double rope through the chain anchor and tossed off the lines. Then he snuck off out of view, relieved himself of the triple espresso he'd quaffed that morning, returned to the rap setup and after telling Hagatha for the tenth time not to worry, made a spectacular Rambo-style exit by jumping out and into the yawning void. He let the rope slide as he free-fell perhaps fifteen feet into the thin mountain air. Then he cranked the doubled rope up against his TCU and jerked to a stop. Immediately he was wrenched upside down.

Staring up at his legs, he saw that the waist belt on his harness had come unthreaded from the buckle, due to the fact that he had not doubled the webbing back through the buckle after taking a whiz on the summit. By shock-loading the rig with his asinine rappelling stunt, he had caused the waist belt to come unfastened. Now the harness had slipped down to midthigh—and was slipping farther and farther down (or rather, up) by the second.

"Holy S#%T, Hagatha!" he shrieked. Dead upside down, dangling some 130 feet above the boulders, Upton folded his legs back and snagged the slipping harness behind his knees. Gasping and shaking dreadfully, Upton fed out an inch of line at a time, certain that if his legs straightened, the harness would shoot off and he'd skydive to the Other Side. After fifty feet his legs were pumping out from the Herculean effort of trying to keep the creeping harness clamped behind his knees. After another twenty feet of inching down, his legs cramped. He trembled, cursed, shouted—and almost screamed as he saw his fried legs straighten and the harness slip out from behind his knees.

Somehow, the harness snagged around his left ankle. Still forty feet off the deck, Upton actually pissed his own britches as he held what felt like his last breath and fed precious inches of line through the TCU. Forty feet became thirty, then twenty . . . but the harness was prying the slipper off his foot. Ten feet off the ground, the slipper shot off, followed by the harness. Death-gripping the rope, Upton swung rightside up. The rope smoked through his hands and he augured in, sustaining bad heel bruises to both feet.

COMMENTARY: There's little question that Upton's mind was much more on his charcoal etchings—and Hagatha's positive reaction to same—than on the rappel at hand. Because rappelling accidents are common and are usually serious, Upton should have tended to business. Also, leaving a novice alone to rig and execute a long and scary free-hanging rappel is dangerous and plain stupid. At the very least Upton should have stayed on top, belayed Hagatha down the rappel, then followed himself.

PREVENTION: ALWAYS check every aspect of the system before committing to even the most straightforward rappel. And always double the webbing on your waist belt back through the buckle.

# 58

# FROZEN IN THE BOMBAY DOOR

*"If he popped, they were both goners . . ."*

Around 1970, Joe Herbst and partner made the first ascent of the Black Velvet Wall at Red Rocks, Nevada, via a spectacular crack and chimney line (5.9) up the 1,600-foot sandstone bastion. Word quickly got out to Yosemite climbers of this wondrous adventure climb, and several made the long trip to Red Rocks to repeat the Velvet Wall masterpiece, a sort of desert Steck/Salathé.

The third ascent was attempted by Ralph, a longtime Yosemite hardman, and his cousin Winchell, who'd spent several summers in the Valley as well, but had fooled away most of that time on the Glacier Point Apron. Though a 5.11 slab climber, Winchell didn't know a chimney from Shinola. The *Herbst Route* up the Velvet Wall was cracks and chimneys most all the way. No matter, said Ralph. If things got bleak, he'd take the sharp end. He could ace 5.9 cracks and chimneys in his sleep.

Ralph and Winchell trudged up to the dark and brooding wall one morning and started up, swinging leads. The first half-dozen crack pitches fell beneath them with little toil. Presently they came to a gaping, bombay chimney. Though rated only 5.7, it looked like death in mineral form. It was Winchell's lead. Since Winchell had cruised the lower crack pitches, half of them on the lead, Ralph encouraged his cousin to go up and "have a look" at the chimney.

Winchell obliged. After forty feet of urgent knee-barring, with the vile flare seeking to puke poor Winchell out on every move, it became clear there was no going down. It also became clear there was no protection. At all. Fearing for his soul, his limbs crooked and slipping between the flaring sandstone walls, Winchell wailed that the topo said nothing about a do-or-die chimney. Scribbled in Crayola on the back of a Keno marker, the topo said little more than where the route started. Winchell pushed on, scrapping, belching, ratcheting, blubbering. Eighty feet out he clasped a huge bucket on the chimney wall where he could stop with complete security, shake his limbs out and get his wind back.

Cousin Ralph yelled up that he'd "handled it like a man." Winchell was only twenty feet short of a big ledge—but that twenty feet looked like more of the same grappling he'd done below. He'd yet to get a nut in, and clearly there were none to be had till the ledge. After ten minutes, Ralph yelled up for

Winchell to carry on "while we're still young." But Winchell couldn't move, or wouldn't move, which amounted to the same thing. Ralph threatened, cajoled and begged—but cousin Winchell wouldn't go.

With no other choice, Ralph finally started up, tied to the other end of Winchell's lead rope. If he popped, they both were goners. A master chimney climber, things went well till Ralph had to pass Winchell—baying and rattling on the big bucket hold. Here he had to work far on the outside of the flare, hanging off marginal arm bars and staring down at the deck some 600 feet below. In time he gained the ledge, brought Winchell up and, with Ralph now in the lead, the pair finished their ascent.

COMMENTARY: "Sandbagging" is a long tradition and involves: A) tricking or goading a person into doing something beyond their abilities, or B) underestimating the difficulty of a climb, with the result of humbling a hotshot or terrorizing a novice. Both versions are the Devil's work, and the consequences can be fatal. A more subtle version of sandbagging is what Ralph did, perhaps unintentionally, to his cousin Winchell: not being straight with him about the obvious difficulties of the route. With Ralph's experience he could take one glance at the unprotected, bombay chimney and realize that a slab climber no more belonged in that ghastly flare than a warthog belongs in a bird's nest. As it often happens, two climbers of different skill levels will team up for a route that is well beyond one of the climber's abilities. The only way this can work is for the more experienced climber to honestly explain what the route will entail, or what is expected. Dragging a novice up a route when he or she didn't have a clue what they were getting into is a fine way to make an enemy. Or get someone hurt.

PREVENTION: How to avoid being sandbagged? If you have any questions, ask around. If the route looks harder or more serious than you've been told, your gut instincts are probably correct. The way to avoid sandbagging someone else is, first, develop a conscience, and second, realize that if you're sandbagging a partner, you'll probably have to compensate for your own deception. At the very least Ralph should have led the obviously dangerous pitches, like he'd promised to.

# 59

# THE SKIES PART ON ORKNEY

*Save a penny, spend a shilling*

Alfred, a British subject, and George, a Scotsman, had rented mopeds and driven to the Kirk Wall, a popular practice crag in northwestern Orkney. Establishing a toprope on the twenty-meter cliff involved scrambling up a rubbly shoulder (fourth class) that flanked the vertical face, then traversing right along the narrow top of the crag to a two bolt anchor. Alfred scampered up the rubbly shoulder, traversed fifty feet right and rigged the toprope presently, tying off the bolts (which did NOT have a sport-climbing chain setup) with locking crabs and a short length of static line which he extended over the lip, clipping the toprope through two more lockers, the gates opposed—all in all, a textbook setup.

Alfred downclimbed and both men made several laps up the wall before an afternoon thundershower began pelting them. The pair's climbing expedition was done, for the wall wouldn't dry out for hours. Alfred once again scrambled up the rubbly shoulder, finding the footing rather treacherous in the downpour. Now on top, he traversed over to the anchors, yelling down to George that he didn't fancy reversing the descent in the pouring rain, but would instead absail off the anchors rather than risk his life downclimbing.

George thought this a prudent decision—till he realized that, since he owned all the gear, whatever Alfred left behind would be his (George's) loss. An affirmed skinflint, a chintzy, tight-fisted cheapskate who prized his possessions above his very soul, George informed Alfred that he *would* again be downclimbing, because, he said, no self-respecting Englishman would forego a challenge and an opportunity for self-improvement.

"Bugger that!" Alfred yelled. He remained dead set on absailing off. But since he had no belay/rappel device on his person and no other gear save that composing the toprope setup (several crabs and the shank of static cord), he shouted down that he'd have to rig something from which George could lower him to the ground—a carabiner would have to be sacrificed. George the skinflint was incensed at the prospect of leaving any gear behind. He wailed, raged, and finally bamboozled Alfred into looping the toprope through a single, half-inch nylon runner threaded through the bolts. Off this, George started lowering Alfred to the deck.

Ten feet from the ground the runner melted through and Alfred the Englishman slammed into the flinty Orkney turf, sustaining tragic bruises to his arse.

COMMENTARY: George demanded that Alfred take a risk that he would never have taken himself. Concurrently with this demand, the Devil was forging a pitchfork with George's name on it. Nevertheless, Alfred was free to choose how he was going to rig his lowering setup—and he knowingly made a dangerous choice.

PREVENTION: Never allow someone to bully you into doing something dangerous. Trust your experience—or at any rate, your instincts. Learn the standard safety procedures and follow them to the letter. The thrill of cleaning a fixed piece of gear, or the dread of leaving something pricey behind, has led many climbers to risk their lives—and some to lose them.

# 60

# JOE SPILLS THE JO

*Nasty burn on Jasper's ass*

Joe and Jasper rose early on the morning of their sixth day on *Tis-sa-ack* (5.10 A4), northwest face of Half Dome, Yosemite Valley, California, United States of America. Bivouacked in portaledges on the long bolt and rivet ladder high on the frightening, black-streaked wall, only three pitches separated the duo from the summit—and only the first of these last three leads (A3) promised any difficulties. Barring an earthquake, a typhoon, or a July snowstorm, the pair expected to top out around noon.

Long-time caffeine addicts, Joe and Jasper began their morning ritual of brewing up several dozen tumblers of espresso prior to their morning constitutional and, eventually, the first lead. Jasper handed the stove up to Joe, whose portaledge dangled just above Jasper's. Joe had a small, foot-square piece of plywood that he placed at one end of his portaledge and on which he set the stove and coffee apparati. The water was just coming to a boil when a crazy hiker (who had bivouacked on the summit) began trundling rocks off the Visor, a huge stone wafer cantilevered off the summit lip some ways above and left of the duo. Though far out of harm's way, the mortar-like WHOOSH! of whistling rocks so startled Joe that he inadvertently booted the stove over. Luckily, most of the scalding liquid spilled into space, but a small amount leaked through the nylon portaledge, burning Jasper's backside.

COMMENTARY: Using a stove on a portaledge requires vigilance. Yet there is oftentimes not a ledge nearby or anywhere else to set the stove on. So if hot beverages are to be had, most climbers are left to cook on their portaledge.

PREVENTION: First, if the portaledges are tiered one on top of the other, the climber in the LOWER ledge should do the cooking to avoid scalding the ass off the other should the boiling liquids spill. Setting a stove straight on the nylon bed of the portaledge is asking for trouble. A little scrap of plywood or plastic—something heatproof that can serve as a platform—is required. And always remember that nylon burns fast and furious. Recall the many incidents of tents going up in flames after catching fire from a stove. Vigilance . . . . And when the "cook" is working, make sure everyone else knows as much and can avoid shifting around and anything else that might jiggle the rigging and set the stove tumbling.

# 61

# 'COURAGE IN A CAN'

*The ground wins . . . again*

Vincent was fresh off a big wall. Early the following morning he staggered over to the picnic tables around "Degan's Deli," the traditional hang for Yosemite hardmen/loafers. Other scoundrels wandered in from scattered and nefarious lairs till a sizable group was assembled and proper drinking could commence. The chosen beverage was Olde English 800, a foul and robust malt liquor, a single can of which is sufficient to twist the lid of the staunchest rummy.

By noon, Vincent had consumed roughly 100 ounces of the vile malt, whereupon he took to his feet and declared himself ready to begin free soloing. According to his friends, there was no question that the Olde English 800, and not Vincent, was doing the talking. Inasmuch as the rest of the crowd was also addled by the malt, there was no one to question Vincent's plans. He somehow managed to wander over to the Church Bowl, boot up and start free soloing *Revisited*, a dicey 5.10. Kevin, a longtime Yosemite wall rat, was nearby and saw Vincent start clawing up the initial holds, following his progress to perhaps the fifteen foot level. The moment Kevin looked away he heard the words, "Oh, Shit!" followed by Vincent's drunken body impacting the deck.

COMMENTARY: Vincent's injuries were so serious that after release from the hospital months later his memory was so poor he had to take notes about things he'd just done and had to do that very day. Climbing has a long heritage of glorifying the hard-drinking cragsman. A hardman is expected to hold his liquor "like a man." (Exceptional women climbers seem to have more sense than to get roped into this macho hooey.) The effort to do so has resulted in the sad and simple fact that many old hardmen are the sorriest kind of drunks, folks of enormous potential who crawled so far into a bottle there was, finally, no getting out. As a young Yosemite regular I climbed under the influence more times than I can remember, and the fact that I'm still alive is proof to me that there is a God. No use preaching. The substance abuser will do as he pleases. I did. But for all those tempted to hit the crags with a load on, how many of you would let a brain surgeon carve on your bean right after huffing a fat reefer or downing ten cans of Olde English 800? The results could be grave. In a sense, climbing is like brain surgery. Life or death choices are made every step of the way. Better to give yourself the edge by having a clear head when making these choices.

PREVENTION: Drinking/drugging and climbing are a fatal mix. Enough said.

# 62

# FROZEN STIFF ON WHITNEY

*Gus flashes back to Hades*

Gus, 50, a Vietnam veteran, and Fatima, 40, a neurologist originally from Quatar, joined a dozen other intermediate climbers for an assault on Mount Whitney in California, the highest peak in U.S. The expedition was organized by a local outdoor equipment retailer who promoted outings for recent grads of their climbing classes, of which Gus and Fatima were alumni. The group had trudged up to the base of the mountain the previous day and bivouacked in a mosquito-tortured meadow some twenty minutes away from the storied east face, which they started up several hours after sunrise.

Despite their "alpine start," the popular *East Face* route was already choked with climbing teams. By the time Gus and Fatima reached midheight on the face, perhaps a dozen or so other teams were in various stages of their ascent, half of that number climbing above the duo. Fiendishly scratching her several thousand mosquito bites, Fatima started across the classic Fresh Air Traverse pitch, moderate but exposed, and had proceeded about fifty feet and placed several pieces of protection when far above rang the dreadful words, "Rock!"

Completely exposed, Fatima could do nothing more than cry, "Allah is great!" and plaster herself against the golden granite wall as a salvo of stones whizzed past. Several dashed the traverse ledge, severing her climbing rope in twain. Securely anchored off, and seeing his beloved's rope smitten in two, Gus could only cower in terror, mumbling to himself in tongues. Fatima maintained her composure, however, and traversed several feet to a fixed piton where she secured herself until another party arrived at Gus's belay stance. Amazingly, no one below was struck by the rockfall. The immediate challenge was not getting a rope to Fatima—a task accomplished in short order—but rather getting the shell-shocked Gus to relinquish his death grip on the anchor and carry on. This task took several hours.

COMMENTARY: "Fight or flight" is one of our deepest instinctual responses. Yet sometimes events happen that are so startling or terrifying that they can short-circuit even our fight- or-flight button, leaving us paralyzed. The potential for this non-response exists in everyone, not just the "weak." For whatever reason, the mind becomes unable to compute an event, and our impersonal, objective energies crash—for a minute or an hour or even longer sometimes. There is little doubt that Gus's episode related to his war experiences—he said as much later—but the reasons matter little in the teeth of the crisis. What matters is getting the person back up to speed and then to safe ground. The trick to resolving such situations is to understand that the rational mind has not been lost; rather, the system has momentarily glitched and you need to reboot in a nonjudgmental, reassuring way.

PREVENTION: There is no real "prevention" for this scenario (which I have seen and experienced myself on several occasions). The secret is knowing how to bring someone back to their right mind. First, make a connection with the person. Let them know that you're there and are going to see the thing through with them; you're not going to abandon them. Next, start with simple things. Have the person tell you their name, then work up to having them count fingers and finally describe where they are and what they are doing. Eventually have them go over what happened. As they start to process the event, stay as connected to them as possible, perhaps holding a hand. The paralysis is caused by the system resisting an experience that it didn't know how to handle; once the resistance is overcome and the experience talked through, the person should regain their balance to the point that you can decide together the next best course of action. Trying to shame a person out of paralysis is certain to make the situation worse.

# 63

# HARD TIMES AT THE HAGGERMEISTERS

*The hatefully hopeless toprope*

A college climbing class met at a practice slab near the Haggermeister Boulders—popular for group instruction—some twenty miles from Boulder, Colorado. Three instructors, each with more than ten years climbing experience, rigged several topropes over the fifty foot slab. The twenty

three students
were all physical
ed majors and had
the fitness to prove it.
One instructor estimated
that every student made over
three laps apiece on each of the
toproped routes before one student, nearing the top of
the right-hand route, slipped off. The anchor failed and
the student tumbled approximately ten feet to the ground,
sustaining multiple bruises.

COMMENTARY: The literature is so full of like versions of this
very scenario that, dull as it might be to read, it would be
irresponsible of me not to spell out the particulars. By far
the most common setup to teach beginners is to string several topropes over a slab, and have the students make as many
laps as possible over the various routes to learn how to trust
their shoes, how to stand on and clasp holds and how to
settle into climbing with a relaxed, upright body position.

This is all good and fine, and there's little risk involved providing safety procedures are followed to the letter and one has a multibolt sport anchor appropriately rigged. Potential trouble enters the equation when natural anchors must be arranged. Owing to the constant weighting and unweighting on the anchor (from all the repeated lowering), camming devices tend to walk into less than ideal positions and other nuts are likewise given to shift, sometimes from bomber placements to worthless ones. For this reason, whenever a natural anchor is used to toprope, instructors are obliged to check said anchor at almost every turn, no matter how bomber the placements. When the activity gets hectic with everyone clawing at the ground to take another lap, the instructors have to have the presence of mind to stop the show momentarily to check the anchors.

PREVENTION: Analysis of this particular scenario revealed that the anchors (three Friends and two hexes) were still perfectly sound; however, to avoid rope drag, a single, knotted, one-inch sling was used to extend the anchor point to the top of the slab climb (a large shelf). Over the course of the day, the overhand knot had worked loose.

This accident was caused by: 1) using an overhand knot to secure the sling, as opposed to a grapevine (or double fisherman's) knot, which virtually never loosens on its own, especially when continuously weighted; 2) a lack in redundancy in the anchor rigging (using more than one sling); and 3) the failure of the instructors to monitor the anchors. Again, when students are making repeated laps up and down a fixed toprope, even the best clean anchors are bound to shift given all the weighting and unweighting. And even if the anchors had been three bombproof bolts, it's always required to keep an eye on the rigging no matter how much redundancy has been engineered into the system.

# 64

# NOT THE KNOT TED NEEDED

*Ted and Alice left high and dry*

Ted and Alice had just completed an ascent of *Stoner's Highway* (5.10) on Middle Cathedral in Yosemite, a divine ten-pitch line of knee-knocking runouts up a creamy swath of bald granite. The route ends at the U-Shaped Bowl, a large, ledgy ramp about 1,200 feet up the face. Here, a team can traverse onto rubbly choss and bash another 1,000 feet to the summit (5.8), or much more commonly, turn round and rap the route — a straightforward business since virtually every pitch ends at a bolted belay fitted with slings from other descents down this fashionable testpiece.

Ted and Alice decided to rap the climbing route rather than continue to the summit. Ted rapped down the third pitch and anchored off to the two-bolt belay with two slings. Alice followed and gained Ted's anchor. Following standard procedure, Ted had tied a "keeper" knot in the end of the rope to avoid rapping off the end while descending a nigh ledgeless ocean of rock. The mistake was that Ted had tied the knot in only one strand of the doubled line. Sure enough, when Alice gained Ted's lower belay anchor, tied herself off with slings and unclipped her ATC from the rope, the strand with the knot in it got away from her, scooted about twenty feet out right and into the plumb line beneath the previous anchor—well out of the duo's reach. Ted and Alice were in a fine mess

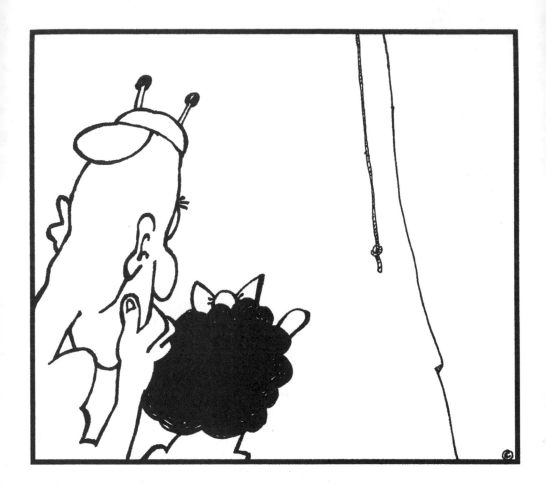

now, for the route went nowhere near the end of the knotted strand, which hung over naked and holdless rock impossible to climb. And the knot was too high for either climber to pendulum for. They had but one option: pull the free end of the doubled rope all the way through the anchor till the knot in the other end arrived at the slings. Hopefully, a few gentle tugs would then pass the knot through the slings and set the rope free. If the knot didn't pass, they would at any rate have pulled an entire lead rope through the anchor, on which Ted could relead the pitch, regain the anchor and rerig the mess.

Ted tugged on the rope and yelled, "Fiddlesticks from Hell!" The line wouldn't budge, and Ted knew why; the knot connecting the two ropes was on the other side of the anchor, the side with the knot in the end of it. Ted pulled like a bull elephant, but the knot connecting the doubled ropes would not pass through the anchor slings a pitch above. Ted, a proud if vain man addicted to self-reliance, grumbled and gritted his teeth in silent fury. Alice, a practical woman not too proud to admit a mistake, put two and two together, slapped a prusik knot on the strand of stuck line and anchored the free end to the bolts. She then re-led the pitch using the prusik for a "belay," back-clipping the rope through the protection bolts en route.

COMMENTARY: I have never before heard of someone tying a knot in only one strand of a doubled rappel rope. Though I have no proof of the results, if a climber hit the knot at speed (during a rappel), I'm not so sure if the climber would stop, or if the rope would not start pulling through the anchors as the knotted and weighted end held fast in the rappel device. In any event, tying a knot in only one strand of the rappel rope is not advised. Had Ted and Alice not been so resourceful, a rescue would have been their only way off.

PREVENTION: Whenever more than one rappel is needed to reach the ground, always tie a knot in the end of the ropes— not in just one strand of ropes, but on both strands. (The reason, of course, is to avoid unwittingly rappelling off the end of the ropes.) A common method is to take the ends of both ropes, fashion a figure-8 knot, and pull it snug. A doubled overhand knot is also used, but it has been known to come untied. Whatever knot you choose should be big enough that there is no chance of it passing through your rappel device.

# 65

# ROY SEES SIGFRIED FLY

*The jugs flew off the rope*

Sigfried and Roy, both longtime wall junkies, had scrimped, borrowed and stolen enough coin to book passage to legendary Baffin Island, Canadian Arctic, to attempt a new route on one of the titanic rock walls rising from this eerie and desolate Disneyland. Once there, the duo trekked far east of the stupendous (4,000 vertical feet) Mount Thor, and after seven days entered a cirque bristling with dozens of virgin granite spires, all unnamed. The pair decided to break in on a 2,500-foot arete, which after visual inspection looked to follow a straightforward crack system suitable for moderate free climbing. In this the Land of Midnight Sun, the pair dusted off 2,000 feet of 5.7 to 5.10 climbing in the first twenty-two hours until collapsing on a big ledge for a little shuteye.

The next "day" passed much the same as the first, with the duo following gorgeous though more vigorous (5.9–5.10d) jamming to where the crack finally pinched off a few leads shy of the snowcapped crown. Roy led a zig-zagging mixed pitch ending just below the summit notch, and belayed in slings. Sigfried followed on jumars. Per standard wall procedure, Sigfried would every so often tie in "short" to the rope, which he accomplished by grabbing the cord just below the jumars and tying an overhand knot which he'd then clip off to a locking biner on his harness. Should both jumars somehow detach from the rope he was jugging, he'd fall not to the end of the

line, but instead stop double the distance to his last loop—
the one that was tied off "short." Smelling the summit,
Sigfried raced up the line, cleaning the pro till he came to
the last placement—a small wired nut ten feet down and
left of Roy's sling belay. Sigfried removed his top jumar
(the right one) and reattached it to the rope above the
nut. The oblique force that resulted twisted the cable
round on the nut, pinning the biner's gate against the rock
and making it difficult to unclip the rope. After several
attempts to unclip the rope from the biner, Sigfried lost
patience. In order to put his full weight on the top jumar
and not swing right, Sigfried stemmed his right foot out
onto a hold and, leaning against the top (right) jumar,

unclipped the lower (left) jumar, intending to clip it onto the line past the cranky biner, then reach back to clean the placement.

Soon as he unclipped the lower jumar, however, his foot popped off the foothold whereas his weight wrenched onto the top jumar, which immediately came detached from the rope. The last time Sigfried had tied off "short" was twenty-five feet below, so he pitched down the wall fifty feet before wrenching to a halt. He hit nothing on the slightly overhanging wall, but during the ride he instinctively grabbed at the rope, sustaining nasty burns to his palms and fingers.

COMMENTARY: Sigfried was able to dress his wounds with ointment and athletic tape and finish the route, but his burns (several fingers were scribed down to the dermis) put a premature end to their expedition after just this one warm-up climb.

PREVENTION: Sigfried was rigged the normal way, with aid slings and daisy chains attached to the jumars, both at appropriate lengths (several inches below one's full reach). However, he made several mistakes. First, whenever you have to fiddle with the ascenders to clean a piece of gear, especially when it's necessary to unclip the top ascender and reattach it on an angling rope or above an abrupt edge/lip, one should always tie off short before doing so. If something goes wrong, you fall only a matter of a few feet. Second, there can be no doubt that when Sigfried reattached the top jumar, the cam was not fully engaged on the rope, because it is extremely unlikely that a properly engaged cam would have come detached. Every climber learns to finesse the ascenders a certain way, and I could spend pages describing the many nuances which, in fact, vary from model to model. The important thing to remember is—whenever there is potential trouble, or whenever you must remove one ascender from the rope, always tie in short so if the worst happens you'll only fall a short ways.

# 66

# LARRY LEAP-FROGS ALOT

*The rusty, manky, mauled and entirely shabby fixed 1" angle came out!*

Larry and Jake were slugging up the breathtaking headwall on the *Salathé Wall*, El Capitan. They'd been on the climb for three days and had made steady progress despite Jake having the previous day dropped a gear sling containing most of their 1" SLCDs (Spring Loaded Camming Devices). The cams were not crucial till the second headwall pitch. Since they were aid climbing (the second headwall pitch goes free at 5.13), the lead required exactly what

Jake had dropped. The pair still had two camming devices that would work in the 1" crack, plus a handful of other chocks which, when placed ingeniously (sideways, etc.) would work— if marginally.

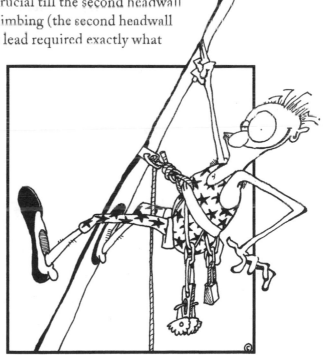

Larry grimaced at his meager rack and started up the second headwall pitch. After thirty feet, he ran out of gear, so he lowered down the overhanging wall some twenty feet, removed his previous four or five placements and returned to his high point. He carried on for thirty more feet till reaching an old, rusty, manky, mauled and entirely shabby fixed 1" angle piton—off which Larry lowered down again, removing the five previous pieces, then pulled/frigged back to the fixed piton and yelled, "Hold me on!" Jake locked Larry off, who leaned back to rerack the gear, pulling directly outward on the old, rusty, manky, mauled and entirely shabby fixed 1" angle piton, which shot from the crack like a toothpick from a cheddar wedge. Larry fell about fifty feet before a #8 Stopper arrested him and he could start leap-frogging all over again.

COMMENTARY: Lucky for Larry the *Salathé Headwall* is over-hanging, so in falling he hit nothing but rarefied air. Because Jake had dropped half the rack on a previous pitch, leap-frogging gear was in fact his only option, but trusting the manky fixed angle was unwise. The headwall crack gobbles nuts. In completing the lead, which required much leap-frogging, Larry lowered off his own placements rather than trusting the manky fixed pegs on the pitch.

PREVENTION: Leap-frogging is a necessary evil when, for whatever reason, you lack enough gear to lead a pitch all the way through. Careful planning can remove the chance of having to leap-frog, but "shit happens" and there's not one experienced wall climber who has not had to back-clean gear on occasion. So long as you understand that by removing gear you are increasing the potential fall, and so long as you only lower off the best available placements, the risks can be managed, though not eliminated.

# 67

# 'DUSTED' ON DESPAIR

*Freddy flails, flops from classic flare*

Freddy and Sal hiked up to Elephant Rock, Yosemite, to scale the classic *Crack of Despair*, a greasy old-school off-width (5.10) that most modern sport climbers avoid like a steady job. Freddy led the terrifying opening pitch, rated 5.7 but closer to 5.10. Sal followed the pitch, then chugged, wrestled and huffed his way up the crux five-inch crack (5.10) above and belayed at the bottom of a claustrophobic chimney some 300 feet long and equally deep. Freddy lost considerable beef on his right knee as he jackknifed up the wicked crack and gained Sal's belay in diminished condition. Freddy felt mortified to think that the climber who first led this pitch, nearly forty years before, was old enough to be his grandpappy. The thought made the short clip-and-go routes Freddy usually climbed seem like the stuff of pansies and posers. But Freddy's shame dissolved when he gaped above, where a dark and vile squeeze chimney shot upwards like a wormhole to Hell.

Because they had already polished off the crux second pitch, Freddy saw no point in brawling the chimney above simply to get to the top. Sal said that if Freddy was "half a man" he'd seize the moment, grab the rack and cast off up the chimney. Freddy said that since he was a full man, he didn't need to. Sal said fine, he'd lead it himself. Understanding he'd never hear the end of it if he let Sal usurp his lead, Freddy changed his mind, grabbed the rack and started squirming up the dark and oily flare. The width was too big for heel and toe jams, too narrow for knee locks, too weird for arm bars—it was in fact the wrong size to do anything but flail on, given Freddy's lack of off-width experience. He felt as though he was falling out on every move.

Ten feet up he actually did fall. He rattled down the flare until both feet crashed onto Sal's shoulders, separating the right shoulder and badly bruising the left. Because Sal was rendered unable to use his dominant right hand, Freddy had to lower him two pitches to the deck, help him to the car and drive him to the clinic.

NOW I UNDERSTAND WHY SOME FOLKS CALL THESE AWFUL WIDTHS!

COMMENTARY: This scenario brings to light several topical issues above and beyond the fact that belayers are well advised to position themselves so a leader cannot fall on their heads. First, popular traditional areas like Yosemite are reporting an increase in accidents among so-called expert climbers. Closer inspection shows that many of these experts are in fact sport-climbing specialists with limited experience handling the special demands of adventure climbing—such as rigging complicated anchors, acquiring adequate protection when it's hard to arrange, route finding on wide open faces where the bolts are few if any, and running the rope out above questionable wired nuts, to mention only a few. Adventure climbing is a game of experience and calculating risks. Also, special techniques, such as wide-crack climbing, cannot be acquired on anything but wide cracks. In fact, the broad strokes of adventure climbing can only be learned while adventure climbing. Lured by lower numbers, sport climbers can be led to believe that the challenges of old adventure climbs can be handled with little if any experience in that arena. The fact is, sport-climbing prowess does not translate into proficiency in "trad" climbing. Working up the adventure-climbing ladder should be done slowly, with the emphasis on safety and control. Unlike most sport climbs, many adventure routes are perilous even when a climber does everything correctly.

PREVENTION: Belaying directly below a leader is dangerous business when the lead is unprotected, as is the case with the third pitch of *Despair*. In a chimney deep as this one, Sal needed only wiggle a few feet left or right to avoid getting fallen on.

# 68

# MIRACLE ON FRUSTRATION

*Yabbo dives for deliverance*

From his earliest days, the late, great John "Yabbo" Yablonski had an atomic-caliber energy that could take hold of him like a demon. If a conniption seized him near a crag he was certain to risk his life doing something crazy. (As his occasional partner I several times wanted to kill him for risking my life as well.) And so it was one blazing summer day that Yabbo found himself at Suicide Rock—without a partner. This was a dangerous situation for Yabbo's person, for he was the kind of soloing maniac who would make the crag live up to its name if he didn't rope up with someone—and quick.

After spending upwards of ninety seconds trying to dragoon a partner (Yabbo had no rope or rack), the energy swelled in Yabbo's loins. He set off jogging along the Buttress of Cracks, searching for an immediate adrenalin blast. Yabbo stalked up to *Frustration* (5.10), the grimmest of these fissures, and booted up. A precarious medley of fingertip layaways and beveled flutes, *Frustration* had hosted roughly 25,000 ascents since the last rains and sported grease enough to lube the fittings of the USS *Midway*. It was a cloudless, midsummer day. The mountain sun beat down like a sledgehammer. The initial stretch of *Frustration*—the crux—seemed to fairly ooze sweat and suet. Yabbo chalked, shuddered and started up. Several gallons of espresso sloshed around his otherwise empty gut, adding a marked urgency to

Yabbo's habitually frantic style. He jittered over the first thirty feet on brute strength, which he had in spades. Just above, the route transitioned from borderline pinches into a bottoming gash, the climbing through this section accomplished by smearing a toe on nothing whatsoever while yarding on a wet bar of Palmolive. Yabbo smeared his toe, clasped the greased hold, started to yank—and realized he was buttering off toward the Land of Harps. Had a witness not been standing by, nobody would possibly have believed the sequence that followed.

Just as Yabbo's toe blew off and the greased hold slipped from his grasp, he torqued his body around to face outward, thrust off the wall with his legs and dove, much as Jalvert plunged into the Seine in the scene from *Les Misérables*. As Yabbo froze Strawberry Valley with a mortal wail, the stunned witness knew she was watching the act of a man gone mad.

Yabbo had vaulted perhaps ten feet away from the wall and fallen the same distance when, Spiderman-style, his arms shot out and his hands snatched the quick of a pine bough drooping from a tree some twenty feet away. Death-gripping the branch, he began to slow down. The branch bowed, popped alarmingly, and—just as Yabbo's decelerated weight touched ground—the stick snapped in two.

"Shucks!" Yabbo scoffed. He pitched the branch aside and, noticing the astonished witness, asked, "Hey, you want to do a climb?"

COMMENTARY: Seventeenth-century French author La Rochefoucauld said that supremely lucky people rarely amend their ways. They always imagine they are in the right when fortune upholds their tomfoolery. Like any large community, the climbing world has always sported a handful of "chosen ones" who can literally get away with suicide. Yabbo was one of these chosen ones, a climber the rock refused to kill. The rest of us are well served in believing the rock is indifferent to our lives and that we must proceed with respect for potential trouble.

PREVENTION: For Yabbo? Professional help was indicated . . . .

# CLIMBING GLOSSARY

**aid:** using means other than the action of hands, feet, and body english to get up a climb

**anchor:** a means by which climbers are secured to a cliff

**arête:** an outside corner of rock

**armbar, armlock:** a means of holding onto a wide crack

**ATC:** stands for Air Traffic Controller, a friction device used to repel and/or belay

**bashie:** a piece of malleable metal that's been hammered into a rock seam as an anchor; used in extreme aid climbing

**batman:** to climb the rope hand over hand

**belay:** procedure of securing a climber by the use of rope

**beta:** detailed route information, sometimes move by move

**bergschrund:** the uppermost crevasse in a glacier

**bight:** a loop (as in a bight of rope)

**biners:** see carabiners

**bollard:** a naturally constructed ice and snow anchor

**bolt:** an artificial anchor in a drilled hole

**bomber or bomb-proof:** absolutely fail-safe (as in a very solid anchor or combination of anchors)

**bucket:** a handhold large enough to fully latch onto, like the handle of a bucket

**cam:** to lodge in a crack by counterpressure; that which lodges; slang for SLCDs

**carabiners:** aluminum alloy rings equipped with a spring-loaded snap gate; called biners

**ceiling:** an overhang of sufficient size to loom overhead

**chock:** a wedge or mechanical device that provides an anchor in a rock crack

**chockstone:** a rock lodged in a crack

**clean:** a description of routes that may be variously free of vegetation, loose rock, or the need to place pitons; also the act of removing chocks from a pitch

**cold shut:** a relatively soft metal ring that can be closed with a hammer blow; notoriously unreliable for withstanding high loads

**crampon:** metal spikes that attach to climbing boots and provide traction on ice and snow

**crimper:** a small but positive edge

**crux:** the most difficult section of a climb or pitch

**deadpoint:** a controlled lunge for a hold

**dihedral:** an inside corner of rock

**drag:** usually used in reference to the resistance of rope through carabiners

**Dulfersitz:** a method of rappelling that involves wrapping the rope around the body and using the resulting friction

**dynamic or dyno:** lunge move

**edge:** a small rock ledge, or the act of standing on an edge

**exposure:** that relative situation where a climb has particularly noticeable sheerness

**fifi:** an un-gated hook used to quickly attach a climber to an anchor

**figure-eight (figure-8):** a device used for rappelling and belaying; or, a knot used in climbing

**free, free climb, or free ascent:** to climb using hands and feet only; the rope is only used to safeguard against injury, not for upward progress or resting

**French technique:** a method of ascending and descending low angle ice and snow with crampons

**glissade:** to slide down a snowfield on one's rump or feet

**gobis:** hand abrasions

**hangdog:** when a leader hangs from a piece of protection to rest, then continues on without lowering back to the ground; not a free ascent

**jam:** wedging feet, hands, fingers, or other body parts to gain purchase in a crack

**jug:** a big hand hold; slang for jumar

**jumar:** to climb a rope using mechanical ascenders

**Jumar:** a brand-name mechanical ascender, used to climb up a rope

**lead:** to be first on a climb, placing protection with which to protect yourself

**lieback:** the climbing maneuver that entails pulling with the hands while pushing with the feet

**line:** the path of weakness in the rock which is the route

**mantle:** the climbing maneuver used to gain a single feature above one's head

**monodoigts:** very small holes or holds, about finger size

**move:** movement; one of a series of motions necessary to gain climbing distance

**nut:** same as a chock: a mechanical device that, by various means, provides a secure anchor to the rock

**on-sight:** to climb a route without prior knowledge or experience of the moves, and without falling or otherwise weighting the rope (also on-sight flash)

**opposition:** nuts, anchors, or climbing maneuvers that are held in place by the simultaneous stress of two opposing forces

**pinkpoint:** to lead (without falling) a climb that has been pre-protected with anchors rigged with carabiners

**pins:** pitons

**pitch:** the section of rock between belays

**pitons:** metal spikes of various shapes, hammered into the rock

**placement:** the quality of a nut or anchor

**protection or pro:** the anchors used to safeguard the leader

**prusik:** a sliding loop of line attached to a rope that locks when weighted

**quickdraws:** short slings with biners that help provide drag-free rope management for the leader

**rappel:** to descend a rope by means of mechanical brake devices

**redpoint:** to lead a route, clipping protection as you go, without falling or resting

**RP:** small nut used mostly in aid climbing

**runout:** the distance between two points of protection; often referring to a long stretch of climbing without protection

**Screamers (Yates Screamers):** load-limiting quickdraws that are sewn in such a manner as to lessen the impact of a fall on protection or anchors

**second:** the second person on a rope team, usually also the leader's belayer

**self-arrest:** a method of stopping a fall on steep snow or low angle ice

**sharp end:** to lead a climb is to take the "sharp end" of the rope

**SLCD:** spring-loaded camming device; lodges in a crack

**sling or runner:** a webbing loop used for a variety of purposes to anchor to the rock

**smear:** to stand on the front of the foot and gain friction against the rock across the breadth of the sole to adhere to the rock

**stance:** a standing rest spot, often the sight of the belay

**stem:** to bridge between two widely-spaced holds

**Supergaiters:** gaiters that enclose the entire boot

**TCU:** Tri-cam unit; a type of SLCD

**thin:** a climb or hold of relatively featureless character

**toprope:** a belay from an anchor point above; protects the climber from falling even a short distance

**trad:** short for traditional climbing or a traditional climber; one who applies "old school" ethics to climbing

**traverse:** to move sideways, without altitude gain

**verglas:** extremely thin ice plastered to rock

**wall or big wall:** a long climb traditionally done over multiple days, but may take just a few hours for ace climbers

**whipper:** a big fall

**yard, or yarding:** to pull; pulling